GW00566501

Buying Horses and Ponies

PELHAM HORSEMASTER SERIES

Buying Horses and Ponies

Elwyn Hartley Edwards

PELHAM BOOKS
LONDON

First published in Great Britain by
Pelham Books Ltd
44 Bedford Square
London WC1B 3DU
1985

British Library Cataloguing in Publication Data

Hartley Edwards, Elwyn
    Buying horses and ponies.—(Pelham horsemaster series)
    1. Horses—Purchasing
    I. Title
    636.1'081   SF285

    ISBN 0 7207 1537 7

Typeset by Action Typesetting, Gloucester
Printed in Great Britain by Hollen Street Press, Slough
and bound by Hunter & Foulis Ltd, Edinburgh

Contents

Picture credits

The photographs are reproduced by kind permission of the following:

Charles Donaldson p. 45
Elwyn Hartley Edwards pp. 60, 155
John Elliot pp. 13, 14, 39, 41, 147
Carol Gibson p. 44
Riding magazine p. 37
W. W. Rouch & Co. Ltd. p. 33
All remaining photographs are
by Leslie Lane

The line drawings are by Desiree White

Introduction

Ever since the early peoples committed themselves to stone tablets on the subject of the horse, and thus, unwittingly, set in motion what was to become an avalanche of equestrian literature, writers of the *genre* have felt impelled to advise their readers on the sort of horse they should or should not buy and how to go about the purchase.

Much of the advice is not all that helpful to the would-be horse-owner of the late twentieth century and a lot of it is positively discouraging, varying as it does from Mr Punch's succinct instruction to the man contemplating marriage – the uncompromising 'Don't' – to John Ward's cynical warning – 'Never believe a word any man says about a horse he wishes to sell – not even a bishop'.

There is little doubt that the word horse-dealer, with the help of so consistently bad a press, has become associated with sharp practice if not with downright dishonesty. Secondhand car salesmen, the natural successors to the old-time horse-dealers, enjoy, or perhaps suffer, from the same image. I don't know much about car-dealers, but so far as the established horse-dealers of my acquaintance are concerned the great majority are just as reputable as people in any other line of business.

On the other hand I have known private persons, good citizens of solid worth and even pillars of the established Church, be quite unscrupulous over the sale of a horse. And there I go, adding my contribution to the largely mythical supposition that buying a horse satisfactorily is an operation beset with every sort of hazard.

In theory the buying of a horse or pony is in its essentials no different from the sale or purchase of any other commodity. In Britain, for instance, the Sale of Goods Act is virtually applicable across the board, and there are similar safeguards, which protect the interests of both buyer and seller, built into the legal systems of most other countries.

In practice, however, it is not always so simple – which is the reason for this book – and the fact that the choice is wide in what, outside of a specific top-performer category, is always something of a buyer's market does not, as might be thought, make it any easier.

In the first place a horse is a sensate creature, never entirely predictable in his actions nor constant in his reactions, performance or outlook. A particular horse may be satisfactory in every way when kept by one person and be far less so when kept by another. It is, therefore, impossible for him to be regarded in the same context as the bag of sugar, the car or the bicycle.

Secondly, there is that all-too-fallible human factor. In a society removed from a horse-dependent economy by a good many generations and conditioned by modern, instant coffee, press-button philosophies, it is not surprising if many horse-buyers, particularly the first-timers, are lacking in experience of what the ownership of horses involves. Keeping a horse, after all, is not the same thing as riding one at a school, however regular that may be. In a transaction involving a living creature the successful outcome depends far more upon the buyer than is the case with the sale and purchase of an inanimate object.

In any sale the law presumes that the purchaser knows

something about the article he is buying, but with a horse you need to know a little more than that. It is necessary, for instance, to have an understanding of the nature of the animal.

There are, of course, sales that go wrong because the vendor is at fault in some way, but in most instances in which a transaction fails to be satisfactory a large degree of blame has to be attached to the buyer, who has failed to equip himself sufficiently well with a background of relevant knowledge.

For all that, however, the exercise of ordinary prudence and taking a few commonsense precautions, including the acquisition of a modicum of basic knowledge prior to rather than after the deal, should result in a perfectly satisfactory outcome.

This book attempts to provide guidelines and a background to the business of buying. Like marriage, the acquisition of an equine partner must always contain the element of a gamble, but the risk of failure is reduced if, in the words of the Prayer Book, the matter is entered into 'advisedly'.

Elwyn Hartley Edwards
Chwilog, 1985

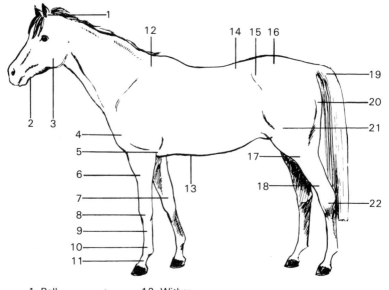

1 Poll
2 Curb groove
3 Gullet
4 Point of shoulder
5 Point of elbow
6 Forearm
7 Chestnut
8 Knee
9 Cannon
10 Fetlock
11 Pastern
12 Wither
13 Girth line
14 Loin
15 Point of hip
16 Croup
17 Stifle
18 Second thigh
19 Dock
20 Point of buttock
21 First thigh
22 Hock

Fig. 1 The points of the horse

1 Suit Yourself

The rage for horses has become a positive epidemic; many persons are infected with it whom one would have credited with more sense.

Lucian (c. AD 125-190)

Having once decided upon the purchase of a horse it is no bad thing to consider the factors governing the choice which will eventually be made.

In simple terms the factors to be taken into account are:

1   The purpose for which the horse is required.
2   The rider's experience and level of competence.
3   The facilities available for keeping the horse, together with the circumstances under which he will be looked after.
4   The price.

All these are interdependent, the choice being influenced by a combination of all four rather than by any particular one.

The **purpose** to which the horse is to be put has an obvious influence upon choice. If we have ambitions to go showjumping or we want to compete in the eventing discipline then we shall need a horse with, at least, the physical potential to take part in what are essentially athletic pursuits. If our purse is long enough it would be an advantage to buy a horse with some experience, but that, in turn, depends to a large degree upon our own experience and competence. In any event we shall need an athletic, even gymnastic, sort of horse with the temperament and courage to match.

If our goal is the Grand Prix dressage test we shall, once more, require strength coupled with athleticism and the temperament that will accept the disciplines of the *manège,* but in this instance we do not need a horse possessed of any speed.

Right at the other end of the scale there is the horse who will be used just for hacking about. He will not need the physical and mental qualities which are essential in the competition horse, but he should have his own particular attributes. He has, for instance, to give a comfortable, on-going ride, his temperament must be the most equable and, above all, he has to be entirely safe in traffic (so far as that is possible with an animal of the horse's nature).

For the majority of riders the requirement is for an all-round, general-purpose horse who does something of everything: taking his turn in the hunting field, perform-ing with reasonable success at the middle level of competition and able to take his rider hacking through the countryside and along the lanes in a good degree of safety and comfort. In fact, this is the most difficult horse of all to find. I had, at one time, a quite superb intermediate event horse. Too small for the big three-day event but otherwise a remarkable little fellow of enormous courage and ability. As a hack, however, he was a misery, constantly falling over himself, spooking at pieces of paper or figments of his imagination, and a penance to ride out. I had another who was a wonderful hack, with the best of manners, but across country he was the most unreliable, chicken-hearted animal you could imagine. Then there was (and is) a little coloured horse. As a showjumper he is hard to fault but he is not the most pleasant horse to take hunting, despite his undoubted jumping ability, nor is he the most pleasant of hacks. One always feels that he is taking you for a ride, which is probably true since his braking and steering systems leave something to be desired.

This one is rather better in front than behind but for all that he became a very good intermediate event horse

The point I make is that only very few horses do everything very well. Like humans, they have their strengths and their weaknesses and we fail in our appreciation of them if we think otherwise.

The purpose for which we buy horses is related to a very considerable extent to our own levels of competence, a matter about which, when we are contemplating buying a horse, we should be ruthlessly honest.

A near Thoroughbred mare who has scope and is the sort to make a good competition horse

It would, for instance, be nonsensical for a novice rider with no pretensions to an equestrian education, to buy a top-flight dressage horse in the mistaken hope that the horse would become a passport to the international arenas. The result could not be more than a disappointed, disillusioned rider and a confused and possibly ruined horse.

The ideal, if we can afford it and find it, is a horse which has been trained to a level which is a step above our own, and thus provides a challenge; *unless,* of course, we ourselves are sufficiently advanced to cope with a horse at either a high level of training, or, conversely, sufficiently experienced to take on a promising youngster and train him on – which is probably the most satisfying thing to do.

The moral is that the more experienced and expert the owner/rider/trainer the wider is the choice – and, of course, the opposite holds true. The less competent the rider the more he is likely to have to pay to find a suitable horse.

In the introduction to this book I likened the purchase of a horse to the choice of a partner in marriage, an analogy that is not as fanciful as it may seem. In a good partnership, either the human one or that between human and horse, a high degree of compatibility is essential.

There is no doubt in my mind about the truth of the assertion that the horse is the mirror of the rider. Neurotic riders produce neurotic horses, bold riders imbue their mounts with their own courage. Sometimes it can be the other way round. For a period in my life I had the reputation of being a bold, thrusting horseman when, in fact, I was just lucky enough to have the most courageous of horses and was no more brave than to go where my good horse would take me. Those, however, are the superlative horses, and we shall be lucky to get more than one or two in a lifetime. For the most part the horse reflects the rider's character, and so if you are set on cutting out the work in the hunting field, but are somewhat less than a bold rider, look for a highly-couraged horse, if you can find one.

If you are a highly strung, intense sort of person (the kind who is sometimes said to be possessed of an 'electric bottom'), don't go for a horse of similar characteristics – you need the more solid, phlegmatic type. There may be something after all in the union of opposites, although so far as horses go the ultimate partnership must be that of the bold, brave horseman on the bold, brave horse.

Perhaps a definition of the words 'experienced' and 'competent' should be attempted at this point.

Frequently, I have been told by fond parents that their twelve-year-old offspring is 'a most experienced horse-woman' – which is rubbish. No twelve-year-old can have lived long enough to become experienced at anything. Unfortunately, in Britain there is still a popular misconception about riding. For some reason, obscure to me, it is thought that riding is no more than a matter of practice. Of course, it is not. Riding, like playing the piano or ballet dancing (or even writing), is an art which has to be learnt; practice is only a corollary of skilled instruction and on its own can lead to virtually ineradicable errors.

I have friends, my old instructors, who are now in their late fifties, or early sixties. For upwards of thirty years these men have ridden six hours a day in every form of riding discipline, having been brought up in the classical mould. They have, in their lives, schooled hundreds of horses and yet they would still claim to be learning. They might rightly be considered as experienced, educated horsemen.

Few of us can lay claim to so high a degree of experience and competence, or can hope to achieve such levels. A very, very few are natural, born horsemen. Some, possessed of courage, get an immediate and commendable result in the short term. But, as a great and wise horseman once wrote: 'Good riding is an affair of skill, but bad riding an affair of courage.'

'Good riding', he continued, 'will last through age, sickness and decrepitude, but bad riding will last only as long as youth, health and strength supply courage.' For 'good riding' he could have substituted 'educated riding'.

In any estimation of our own experience and competence, and certainly of that possessed by young people, it would be as well to err on the side of caution – particularly when the latter are becoming importunate in their demands for expensive equine additions to the household.

(There is another definition of experience, related to me by a forward young lady of my acquaintance. 'Experience', she said, 'may, in the end, become the comb you find in your hand when you have already gone bald!')

A factor which requires the utmost consideration when buying a horse is that of the **facilities** available for keeping it.

Under the collective term facility has to be included: pasture, stabling, storage areas (for feedstuffs, bedding etc) and the finance available for feed, equipment, transport, shoeing and veterinary attention.

Pasture
It is not impossible to keep a horse without a paddock, but it involves stabling for the greater part of the year and the hire of suitable pasture on which the horse can be put out for a holiday, as it were, for a short period. Many horses live quite satisfactorily in this way, and in the past such an arrangement would have been common-place for horses working in urban areas.

The advantage of a paddock is that, so long as it is large enough and properly managed, it will provide some feed during part of the year. It may, again depending on its size, provide all-the-year-round accommodation for a horse kept on a living-out system, or at least summer grazing for horses stabled during the winter. For stabled horses it can also be used as a running-out area in which the horses, fitted with waterproof New Zealand rugs, can be turned out for a few hours a day. Keeping horses in this way (it is sometimes called the combined system) is claimed to be labour-saving – which it is not since horses turned out in this fashion get themselves incredibly dirty. On the other hand the system has definite advantages. Horses that cannot be ridden out every day can exercise themselves. Furthermore, running out at liberty for a few hours daily allows horses to 'unwind' mentally and prevents their becoming bored. A paddock is, therefore, a very useful facility.

Its usefulness, however, is dependent on its size, its management and the subsequent quality of the grazing.

It is just possible with a stable and very good management to keep a horse on one acre but for me two acres per head would be a more acceptable minimum.

Two well-drained acres, harrowed annually, regularly cleared of droppings and fertilized twice a year, will provide sufficient summer feed for a pony or possibly for a horse, but at some point during the year the ground will need to be cleaned up by topping, or by putting cattle on it to eat off the rough patches (horses are notorious as the worst of selective grazers) and to prevent the land becoming worm-infested and horse-sick. Horses kept out in the winter on this sort of acreage will require substantial supplementary feeding if they are to remain in good working condition. If they are doing no work they will still need to be fed a generous ration of hay.

Of course, a paddock has to have a supply of, preferably, running or piped water, or be so conveniently sited as to allow for water to be supplied in buckets. It needs also to be safely fenced (preferably not with barbed wire) and, where animals are kept out, to have a field shelter.

Stabling

For horses in regular work, hunting in the winter or competing seriously in the summer, stabling is a necessity. If it is not already included in the property, suitable buildings can be erected if there is sufficient space and if the local authority will grant permission. In urban and some green belt areas this last can be a difficulty.

One then needs somewhere to store feed, hay and bedding materials, as well, ideally, as somewhere to keep saddles, bridles, etc.

Finance

Money, quite a lot of it, will be required for the purchase and maintenance of *equipment*. A stabled horse, which presumably is working and would therefore be clipped in the winter, requires as a minimum: a blanket; a top-rug; a New Zealand rug, if he is turned out at all; leg bandages for travelling; headcollar and lead rope; grooming equipment; saddle mounted with leathers, irons and girth; and a bridle. A veterinary chest needs also to be kept and then there are the extras like tail bandages, exercise boots, travelling knee and hock boots, and even, perhaps, clippers.

Feed is also a major item. Prices vary from one part of the country to another and in our inflationary times are not sufficiently constant to be worth quoting. However, the total daily intake of a horse, bearing in mind that individual consumption is subject to variation, corresponds with the following table.

Height (hh)	12-13	13-14	14-15	15-16	Over 16
Approx. daily intake (lb)	16-18	20-22	22-24	24-26	26-28

Stabled horses in moderate work would be expected to receive half of the total ration as concentrates (ie oats, bran, barley, nuts etc.) and the other half as hay. For horses in hard work the hay ration is reduced to one-third of the total intake, the concentrate being increased accordingly.

Bedding is again a variable factor but allowance has still to be made for it. It will take approximately four bales of straw to make a good bed in a box measuring 12ft × 12ft and one can expect to use two bales per week thereafter. Four bales of shavings are needed for a similar bed, topping up being at the rate of approximately one and a half bales per week. When shredded or diced paper is used a similar number of bales is required initially, and perhaps one bale a week afterwards.

Transport—If the horse is to hunt or compete some form of transport is needed. A trailer is probably the cheapest and there are models which can be towed behind an average size car of 1600cc upwards. Even trailers, however, require regular maintenance, for which allowance must be made. Transport can, of course, be hired, but it is expensive if used with any frequency.

Shoeing—Generally, one would expect to fit new shoes every five weeks on a horse doing some road exercise.

Veterinary—Hopefully only a minimum of veterinary attention will be required, but a sum should nonetheless be allocated when making a budget. Under this heading one includes worm doses, not less than twice a year for mature horses and possibly twice that number of treatments if the worm burden is a heavy one at the commencement, or if the grazing area is dirty and somewhat horse-sick. Allowance also has to be made for the influenza and/or tetanus injections and it would be foolish not to take these precautionary measures. Proof of a 'flu injection is a requirement at most major shows and events. Even if you have insurance which covers vet's fees you will find there is a quite high excess, so allowance still needs to be made for the cost of routine visits. At the outset, therefore, it is advisable that the new horse-owner prepares a budget which gives him some idea of his on-going commitment. The cost of a horse does not, unhappily, stop at the purchase price.

If one does not have facilities at home for keeping a horse there are, of course, alternatives. Grazing and stabling can be rented. When this is done it is better, if it is at all possible, to enter into a properly drawn up legal agreement with the landlord. The agreement can then stipulate the responsibilities of both parties: who is to be responsible for the maintenance of fencing, the arrangements for fertilizing, harrowing, weed control and so on.

The remaining alternative is to keep the horse at livery at a reputable stable, and there are various systems available. Some stables operate a 'DIY livery', others may do part-liveries and grass liveries as well as a full service which involves looking after the horse entirely. It is, of course, always as well to find out exactly what a full livery, or indeed any other sort, actually includes before entering into an arrangement.

I would suggest that the headings for the horse-owner's budget should be on these lines, allowance, of course, being made for individual variations:

Cost	Livery, if required
Per Annum	Concentrate feed
	Hay
	Bedding
	Saddlery and equipment
	Veterinary allowance
	Shoeing
	Insurance
	Transport
	Fertilizer/weed control etc

If you really want to frighten yourself you can add your British Horse Society subscription, your Riding Club and Hunt subs, entry fees, and so on. The list is nearly endless. (Once I had my accountant do a costing on the horses. He included dilapidations, depreciation and a whole lot of other things. Amazingly, considering the awful shock, I still keep horses.)

Price
Finally there is the price to think about, and this will be affected by a variety of considerations not the least of which will be the figure one can afford to give. Otherwise, the principal factors involved, not necessarily in the following order, are: conformation and appearance; performance ability and/or record; weight-carrying capacity; age; and manners. Soundness should never be a point at issue, since nobody, one hopes, in his right mind would knowingly buy an unsound horse. Anyone who does may well have time to repent his purchase at leisure – it will certainly be among the most expensive he has ever made.

If price is not a consideration the problems inherent in finding a suitable horse will be reduced considerably. But for most of us price is a matter of some account and those with limited finance may find the horse of their dreams outside their price range. Nonetheless, there are many good horses to be bought if one is prepared to turn a blind eye to what in a perfect world would count as deficiencies.

A good dealer friend of mine used to say: 'It depends what you want for your money. If he's the right price and does the job you may have to overlook one or two little things.' To what extent one is prepared to overlook may, indeed, depend on the horse being 'the right price'. Splints, for instance, are unimportant and quite a number of jumpers display curbs. Indeed, one might get a very good horse at a little less money if he showed evidence of having sprained a back tendon and check ligament, for he would be likely to continue to give good service. But a horse that has 'broken down' (a term used to describe the rupture of the suspensory ligament) would not be a good prospect. His use would probably be restricted and his price would or should reflect his limitations. All else being equal, I would buy a horse that had been operated on for an affection of the wind, a technical unsoundness for the show ring, or even one that made the suspicion of 'a noise'. The argument is that the horse which has undergone an operation must have been pretty well thought of by his owner for the latter to go to that trouble, whilst the horse that is just a little noisy in his respiration can usually be kept going pretty satisfactorily, and can, of course, be operated on if it became necessary. Because of his technical 'unsoundness' he should not be so highly priced. In any instance where the taking of a little risk of this nature is contemplated, however, it would be unwise to proceed without the benefit of veterinary opinion, which should in any event be sought.

I have had more than one such horse. From this particular friend I bought a little horse who certainly had 'one or two little things' to overlook. He dished in front like the proverbial food mixer and he had a pair of hindlegs which encouraged an extraordinary agility in his handlers. It was not that he was vicious but he did become impatient as he got fit. Nonetheless, despite his lack of size he was the most wonderful performer across country and became the very respectable intermediate eventer mentioned at the beginning of this chapter.

I had another, a mare, bought cheaply because of her condition and her deep dislike of blacksmiths and all their works. She had a head as long as a coffin, and less pretty to look at, but she never turned it away from the biggest obstacle, and in time we effected a suitable compromise about the shoeing problem – we shod her feet two at a time, with a couple of days interval between the sessions.

Conformation, discussed at length in a later chapter, is important because in theory and also, I believe, in practice, the symmetrical horse with straight, matched limbs and correctly formed joints will be better balanced and less likely to suffer strain and sprain. In brief, the well-proportioned horse offers a more efficient structure which should result in an improved performance.

Admittedly, conformation is only one side of the coin. There have been splendid horses of near-perfect proportions who lacked the all-important mental outlook which results in a horse cooperating willingly with human beings in what the latter consider to be normal, even natural pursuits but which the horse can hardly be expected to see in the same light. Such a one was a Royal Dublin Horse Show champion some years ago. He was bought for a very large sum to go jumping but as he declined firmly to launch himself over anything higher than a ground pole he finished his days, poor fellow, drawing a water-cart.

Lucinda Green with the Badminton Horse Trials winner George. Although not the most perfect equine specimen, he had a remarkable ability

Not perhaps a very prepossessing fellow but one of the world's greatest showjumpers. This is Ryan's Son

Another exception, which one must conclude goes towards proving the rule, is the occasional brilliant horse who performs wonderfully whilst exhibiting conformational faults which should by their nature prohibit top-class performance or, at least, be a cause of such unsoundness as to prevent the star quality being in evidence for very long. But they are exceptions and on the whole it must always be in the purchaser's interest to buy the best-made horse that he can find within his price range. The better the conformation, and, therefore, the greater the horse's potential, the higher will be the price. Later, in the chapter devoted to conformation and action, the acceptability or otherwise of minor conformational deficiencies is discussed as well as the different types of conformation which make horses more or less suitable for particular purposes.

At this point a word about blemishes is apposite. Blemishes are disfigurements which may be no more than honourable scars. They can be somewhat unsightly but they do not constitute an unsoundness and if the horse is otherwise a good performer and is not required for the show ring, their presence does not have too great an effect upon price. Splints, those bony enlargements on the inside of the forelegs, would also not be too great a drawback in similar circumstances although, obviously, the horse which is free from any sort of disfigurement should command a commensurately higher price. One might, however, be justified in enquiring what an eight- or nine-year-old hunter had been doing all his life if there was not a mark on him!

Performance has an obvious effect upon price: a horse with ability and a good track record will make more than will a less successful or less experienced one. The value of 'potential', a word much used and often incorrectly in horse advertisements, is less easily evaluated, since one is being asked to pay not for proven performance but for a promise of future performance. It could be applied with relevance to a completely unproven youngster of classical physical appearance, or to a young horse doing well after, say, a year's schooling. But too often its use is more an expression of pious hope than of anything else.

When, in the course of time, the object of the British Horse Project becomes a reality, the hit-and-miss element in buying will one imagines be reduced considerably. When the breeding and performance of sire and dam, as well as that of other progeny and relations are recorded then it will be possible to make some assessment of potential. Until then the word is best treated with caution. (The British Horse Project seeks to produce a fully documented 'competition horse' – the British Horse Society and the relevant breed societies are cooperating to this end.)

Since young people, we are told, are now bigger and heavier than before, horses that have the ability to carry weight, and to do so comfortably, safely and at speed, often over fences, without their being put at risk in terms of strains and sprains, are likely to be even more in demand than they are today – and probably just as difficult to find.

In general terms the ability to carry weight is concerned with the overall substance and build of the animal (not with the height) and with the bone formation of the lower limbs. The usual guide to the weight-carrying capacity is the diameter of the 'bone', measured below the knee. It used to be said that a horse with 8ins of bone would be up to 11-12st, 9-10ins up to 13-14st and 10-11ins up to 15st and over. But this formula takes no account of the nature of the bone, nor of the fact that any measurement is taken around what is a composite structure of ligaments, tendons and tissue covering bone. The strength of bone is in the density and substance of the material surrounding the bone's central core. The strongest bone is that with the smallest core and the thickest surrounding wall, but, of course, there is no way of determining the nature of the bone by external examination.

Nonetheless, whilst arguments about bone and its nature will continue for as long as people ride horses, there is general agreement that to carry weight horses need the strongest of limbs and *plenty* of bone and substance. It is also agreed that the heavyweight horse of quality (refinement if you like) is expensive because of his rarity and thus big men in search of a suitable horse must expect to pay high prices.

Clearly, the lightweight has the edge in the matter and a wider variety of choice too.

Height is rather less important in influencing price but is something to be taken into account by the rider. There is no point in someone as short-legged as myself buying a big horse which spreads my legs out at right angles and thus diminishes my control and security, any more than it would be sensible for a long-legged rider to 'under-horse' himself with something too small.

Age is without doubt a significant factor in pricing a horse. (The age of Thoroughbred stock, incidentally, is calculated from 1 January in each year and from 1 April for other horses.) Nonetheless, there is no way of calculating specific differences in value solely on the basis of passing years. There is no *Glass's Guide* for horses as there is for cars. In general terms one could say that an animal of two or three that has not been schooled under saddle must be cheaper than one of a similar quality of four to five years, who has been trained. A horse is usually termed mature at six years, when he has a 'full mouth', that is a mouth of permanent teeth, but, of course, there will be exceptions. The full mouth is a convenient demarcation line between spring and summer, as it were, but some breeds and individuals are much slower to mature in the full physical sense. This is certainly true of many big horses who need extra time to grow into themselves and to achieve balance and coordination. Arab horses frequently mature late and so do the Lipizzaners of Austria's Spanish Riding School. Both, however, are long-lived and many of the Lipizzaner stallions are still performing the demanding exercises of the *haute école* at an advanced age.

For all that, a horse is probably increasing in value from the time he begins to work up to the age of eight, thereafter the graph will level off until at about 10 or 11 years the value begins to decline, the speed of the decline becoming more marked in subsequent years. There can, of course, be no hard and fast rule. It could be possible for the value of a horse to rise very considerably after the age of eight if there was a notable improvement in the performance level after that time.

In practical terms a year or two one side or another is not of any great consequence in itself, what is of far more concern is the sort of life the horse has led during those years. A six-year-old horse who has done a lot of competition work, galloping and jumping, and has in consequence been exposed to considerable wear and tear in terms of limbs, joints and possibly his back too, could be a less attractive buy than a nine-year-old who has not been worked so hard.

Similarly, an older horse which was not broken until four, rather than the more customary age of three, and was then ridden on quietly and allowed to develop his full physical potential could be more valuable than a five-year-old broken at two, before he was, perhaps, physically and mentally prepared for work.

Within reasonable bounds, good management from birth onwards is of far more import and value than actual age.

Finally, in assessing the price to be paid, or, indeed, the suitability of the horse for a particular individual, consideration has to be given to what may be called manners when not being ridden, by which is meant general behaviour in the stable and when being groomed, clipped, shod etc, and the ease with which a horse can be boxed for travelling and, very importantly, the animal's deportment on the roads and in traffic.

In some respects this aspect of the horse can be a matter of one man's meat and another man's poison. Fit, highly couraged horses can be gingery and impatient in the stable, sometimes making play with teeth or raising a leg, but this sort of behaviour, so long as it remains manageable and within the compass of ordinary competent people, can hardly be sufficient reason for a reduction in price. In the other respects only a failing which could cause a definite restriction of use could be expected to have an effect upon the price of the animal.

2   Breeds and Types

Buy a horse as you would choose a wife – with circumspection. . .

In Europe and more particularly in Britain, which has a greater variety of native ponies than anywhere else in the world, the choice of breed and type open to the buyer is wide. Indeed, as the horse world becomes increasingly international in its outlook the choice becomes ever greater. Europe, for instance, is committed to the production of the warm-blood competition horse bred selectively on the basis of performance and temperament as much as on conformational excellence and freedom from hereditary disease.

The term 'warm-blood' is applied in Europe to light horse crosses containing elements of 'hot blood', ie Arab or its most notable derivative the Thoroughbred, and in the case of many the influence of the latter is substantial.

In Britain a different terminology is used. A cross between a Thoroughbred and a horse of unknown ancestry or of any breed other than Thoroughbred or Arab, is termed 'half-bred'. Should a half-bred mare be put to a Thoroughbred stallion the resultant progeny is then described as 'threequarter bred', whilst a further cross to Thoroughbred would produce a horse described as 'seven-eighths bred'.

Anglo-Arab, in Britain, is used to describe the progeny of a Thoroughbred horse and an Arab mare, or vice versa, and the products of subsequent recrossing. In other words there is nothing in the pedigree other than Thoroughbred or Arabian blood.

It is different in France, a country which has made a speciality of the Anglo-Arab. To qualify for inclusion in the French Arab Horse Stud Book an Anglo-Arab must have 25 per cent pure Arab blood and have no ancestors in the pedigree other than Arab, Anglo-Arab or Thoroughbred.

'Part-bred', another British term, refers to a horse or pony that can claim some relationship with an established breed, the exact degree being laid down by individual breed societies. There can be, therefore, part-bred Arabs, Dartmoors, Welsh etc.

In addition to the European warm-bloods, the Hannoverians, Holsteiners, Trakehners, Danish, Dutch, Swedish and French horses (the latter going under the name of *Selle française*) there are in Britain, for instance, some of the American breeds like the Morgan and the American Quarter Horse. The more exotic American products, like the Saddle Horse, the Tennessee Walker and so on are not usually seen in Europe and are not really relevant to our horse activities.

With the choice being almost confusingly large it is as well to think about the merits of the specific breeds and types individually, even if that can be done in only general terms.

Thoroughbred

Pride of place must go to the Thoroughbred, the ultimate racing machine and without doubt the essential element in the competition riding horse.

The best Thoroughbred is probably the nearest thing to equine perfection, but it is as well to remember that the second- and third-rate can be as bad, or worse, as those occupying similar categories in other breeds. The desirable characteristics of the Thoroughbred, other than speed, are endurance, stamina, near-perfect balance and above all courage. It used to be said that an ounce of blood was worth a pound of bone, and that is as true as ever it was, but that most desirable of attributes can at the same time be both a strength and a weakness in the Thoroughbred horse.

A Thoroughbred in racing condition

The Thoroughbred needs to be matched by a horseman or woman of similar quality if the partnership is likely to be a successful one. High courage, hot blood and heightened reactions can result in a correspondingly sensitive temperament and it is a fact that for most of our modern equestrian disciplines many pure Thoroughbred horses are not sufficiently equable in their outlook. There are exceptions, of course, and there are riders gifted enough to delight in the Rolls-Royce performance of such horses.

Additionally, the Thoroughbred can be delicate in constitution, more prone to unsoundness and frankly more difficult to keep than his less aristocratic kinsfolk. He rarely, for instance, is able to winter out and may not even do well if turned out in a New Zealand rug. If the horse has raced one has to remember that, although the Thoroughbred is bred and reared for early maturity, his limbs and joints will have received considerable wear from the age of two years. Nonetheless, a percentage of

A Thoroughbred pony stallion who is very hard to fault

Thoroughbred blood is in my view an essential in a riding horse. Opinions will vary as to how much is needed and what is the best amalgam. My own ideal is the threequarter-bred horse with a background of pony blood – Welsh, Connemara, New Forest, Highland or whatever – or with some Irish Draught, Cleveland or even a *soupcon* of cart blood in the ancestry.

Such mixtures act as a leavening to the hot temperament, adding bone, substance and often, in the case of the pony infusions, the characteristic hardiness and qualities of soundness and sagacity which are not always present in the bigger horses.

The Anglo-Arab. This horse is particularly noteworthy for his splendid front

In discussing the Thoroughbred crosses the *Anglo-Arab* cannot be ignored. In Britain Anglo-Arab breeding has never been promoted sufficiently but there have been some very good horses of this crossing, whilst the French Anglos have proved themselves time and time again at the highest level of international competition.

Theoretically, the straight mix of Thoroughbred and Arab should produce the best of both worlds: the speed and size of the Thoroughbred being combined with the kind temperament, hardiness and hereditary soundness of the Arab. The French may, indeed, after nearly 200 years of selective breeding, have come close to the ideal, but with notable exceptions that is not so in Britain where breeding has been with a few individuals, has often tended towards the haphazard and where, in this area as in others, there has never been sufficient emphasis upon performance. Today, however, there are more Anglo-Arabs available in Britain than ever before.

Arabian

The pure-bred Arabian, in Britain at least, is rarely viewed seriously as a performance horse by the majority of horse people, or even by many of those who breed him. The fault, indeed, belongs more probably to the breeders than the horses, for there is no denying that British breeders, whilst producing beautiful stock, have very much neglected the riding/performance factors. That certainly was so in the past; today strenuous efforts are being made to correct the balance.

The good pure-bred Arab despite, or perhaps because of, his lack of size, is without any doubt a very lovely riding horse. However, he rarely goes beyond 15 hh, the ideal being about 14.2 hh. As a result he has limitations. He is not the biggest of jumpers, for example, and for

A pure-bred Arab gelding proving the breed's jumping ability

showjumping or eventing an Arab would not be a good choice. There is no reason why he should not compete in dressage tests, but it has to be recognized that he has immediate disadvantages. In Europe there is still a deeply ingrained prejudice against the breed and the rather different, floating beauty of the Arab in movement is often lost on judges whose eyes are attuned to the powering, earth-pounding action and submissive accuracy of the big and heavily built Hannoverian, for instance.

As a hack, the pure-bred Arabian is infinitely comfortable, striking in appearance, and can be the lightest and most gay of rides (the last adjective being used in its proper sense). As a long-distance horse he is probably unrivalled and as a fun horse at a modest level he is probably better than most. He is pretty easy to keep, notably sound of wind and limb and is claimed to have a temperament combining courage and fire with great gentleness and kindness. Furthermore, the pure-bred Arabian, together with his immediate derivatives, offers the only opportunity for the amateur to ride in races on the flat. The British Arab Horse Society runs regular meetings throughout the summer months and they are becoming increasingly popular. From personal experience I would say that whilst the claims of his admirers can be largely substantiated, the Arab needs a rider possessed of a sense of humour who will, on occasion, not resent taking the junior position in the partnership, and one that is not too competitively minded.

The Arab is claimed to be the most comfortable of riding horses

The Arab influence is evident in this very fetching little horse, who would be a good sort for a lightweight

It is possible that the very popularity of the Arabian, particularly amongst his less critical (and usually less knowledgeable) admirers, acts against the breed's best interests. There are, it is true, bad examples of every type of breeding but few are more noticeably awful than a bad Arab or part-bred, and there are rather too many of the latter.

In my corner of Wales, for instance, which is not noted as an area steeped in horselore, the poorest sort of Welsh scrub stock will more often than not be crossed with the nearest Arab stallion, only a few of which should in any case have been kept entire. It is not by any means the fault of the stallion, of course, (almost invariably referred to as 'Thoroughbred-Arab' in tones of awe) but the progeny can hardly help but be unbelievably poor.

Of course, there are many useful part-breds – one of them won Badminton and another was one of the world's great showjumpers – but for my part I would be looking for something of the order of 50 per cent Thoroughbred with a pony background, perhaps, as well as an Arab one.

Mountain and Moorland

For those who want economy combined with easy management, good temperament and a willing all-round performance at about Riding Club local level or possibly above that, there is nothing like one of the native ponies, the Mountain and Moorland breeds indigenous to these islands.

The larger native ponies: the New Forest, Welsh Cob, Highland, the Connemara and the less well-known Dales and Fell, will all carry an average-size adult and are ideal for all the family. All these ponies stand at 14 hh and above and the Welsh Cob, Dales, Fell and Highland are up to a great deal of weight.

Their origins on the wild mountain and moorland areas, where the terrain was incredibly rough, feed scarce and climatic conditions harsh, have developed in the native breeds qualities which have been largely lost in the bigger horses, bred and reared in softer, less arduous circumstances.

The native ponies are hardy, very sound, particularly in the feet, limbs and wind, and are possessed of excellent constitutions which allow them to survive and even thrive on minimum rations. Their 'pony character' gives them a sagacity and intelligence not possessed by their larger brethren and they usually have the very best of temperaments, being biddable and sensibly cooperative.

Taking them individually, there is the *New Forest,* of

which breed the modern type is a true riding sort with a good shoulder. They are excellent, free-moving performance ponies and they are easily schooled to harness. Upper height limit is 14.2 hh.

There are really two sections of *Welsh Cob*. Section D in the Stud Book is for the bigger cobs over 13.2 hh, many of which can stand as much as 15.2 hh. The smaller Cob, Section C in the Stud Book, is the Welsh Pony of Cob Type with a height limit of 13.2 hh.

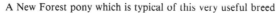

A New Forest pony which is typical of this very useful breed

The Welsh Cob is an enormously strong animal with substance, plenty of bone and, like all the Welsh breeds, the best feet in the business. Without doubt, the Cob

The famous Welsh Cob under saddle

does not lack 'fire in the belly' but he is amiable enough and easily trained. He goes with some knee action and with notable engagement of the hocks, as do many native breeds, having developed that way of going over rough terrain which precluded any low, daisy-cutting types, and he moves with great power overall. Most of them are good jumpers and though they are not the best gallopers in the world they are great performers across anything other than a big, grass country. The Cob, of course, is also an ideal harness horse and has achieved great distinction in this field right up to the level of international competitive driving.

For many years the *Highland* pony, who is a favourite with trekking centres, was considered 'not to be of riding type', a misconception strongly supported by some of the lumpier, more carty Mainland types. No

The Highland, so long as it is not too heavy, is a wonderful stamp of riding pony

distinction is now drawn between the heavy Mainland sort and the lighter Western Isles pony (which was of riding type) and the really heavy sorts are not now so much in evidence. They make good, sensible family ponies that jump well and they are very suitable for beginners, being gentle, docile and reliable. They go to 14.2 hh and are up to any weight.

The *Connemara* is indigenous to Ireland but is bred extensively in Britain and also in Europe. It is, I think, the supreme performance pony and since it can be as big as 14.2 hh it is well-suited to the lightweight adult. The breed has enormous jumping ability and, like all ponies and nearly all Irish horses, appears to be possessed of an inherent genius at crossing a country.

The *Dales* pony of North Yorkshire was at one time

The Connemara is suitable for light adults as well as children. The breed is noted for its jumping ability

influenced by the Welsh Cob – the nineteenth-century trotting stallion Comet, for instance, exerted a very considerable influence. Bred as a pack and harness pony and at one time used for carting lead and coal over the rough Dales country, weight is no problem to this pony. He stands up to 14.2 hh and he is so calm in his temperament that he makes an ideal mount for all the family, and, of course, he will take to harness like a duck to water. His action, like the Welsh Cob, is relatively high but he is said to be a good, reliable performer within his limitations and a clever jumper over reasonably sized obstacles.

The *Fell,* bred on the northern side of the Pennines, is closely related to the Dales pony but is finer and not quite so big, the breed standard is 14 hh. In my view, the Fell has by far the better riding shoulder and in consequence a better riding action whilst still retaining the characteristics of strength, constitutional toughness and good temperament.

The Fell pony from the North of England makes a good mount for both children and adults

Close relative of the Fell is the Dales pony, a strong enduring mount who also excels in harness

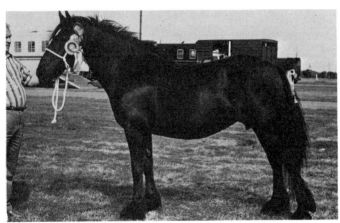

The smaller native ponies, the *Welsh, Dartmoor, Exmoor* and *Shetland,* are discussed in Chapter 10, which is devoted to the choice of a child's pony.

Whilst the Mountain and Moorland ponies are good all-round riding propositions in their own right they have enormous value and potential as the basis for a cross with Thoroughbred blood.

A first cross with all of them, with perhaps the possible exception of the Dales pony, will produce a good sort of cut-and-come-again hunter of medium size which retains the quality of bone and substance and something of the pony character and movement.

A second cross with the Thoroughbred increases the size and scope and is no bad mix for the top-level competition horse.

Crosses from all these larger Mountain and Moorland breeds, with, I think, the exception of the Dales pony, have achieved the greatest distinction in dressage, eventing and showjumping.

Two of the best horses I ever rode in the hunting field were a Thoroughbred/Connemara cross, with the Scarteen in Ireland, and a Thoroughbred/Welsh Cob cross with the Isle of Man Draghounds. Both retained a little knee action, never a bad thing in a crosscountry horse which needs to make adjustments in its stride both on the flat and in the approach to fences, and both were as clever as cats and very athletic. Athleticism and a gymnastic ability are, indeed, prime requirements for the competitive performance horse and they are usually present in these Thoroughbred/Mountain and Moorland crosses.

Warm-Bloods
The Continental warm-bloods are, of course, the product of judicious crossing using the upgrading

Thoroughbred blood to give speed, size, scope, greater fluency of action etc, on a selected base which provides bone, substance, temperament etc.

Unlike the British system, which depends upon the private enterprise and inclination of numbers of small breeders, Continental breeding is, in general, far more organized. There are the large state-supported studs, adequately financed, where selective breeding policies are followed to produce horses for the specific purpose of competition. Great emphasis is laid upon performance, the records of sire, dam, their relatives and progeny being given particular attention. In many instances performance testing of potential breeding stock plays an important part. This is breeding by genotype, if you like, in a conscious effort to eliminate the imponderables so far as is possible. It is playing at being God as scientifically as we know how. In Britain there is now a significant movement, through the formation of the British Horse Project, away from our rather more hit-and-miss methods of largely pheno-type breeding (ie breeding by appearance without too much knowledge of the genetical background) and towards the Continental methods.

As a result of the introduction of warm-blood horses and their undoubted success in many fields there is in some areas a tendency to denigrate the British product – a peculiarly Anglo-Saxon failing, you may think. This is unfair and takes no account of the enormous achievements made by small British breeders. If, for instance, we look at the Premium Stallion scheme operated by the National Light Horse Breeding Society (HIS) it is easy to see that our national product compares very well in terms of quality with that of any other country and is, indeed, considerably better than most. Bear in mind, too, that Britain has a greater number of active riders at every level, per capita of the population, than any other nation in the world, the very great majority riding horses produced in this country.

The National Light Horse Breeding Society stallions are Thoroughbred horses which are offered to members at a service fee which is far less than the market rate, and all are free from hereditary disease. Their progeny, usually from non-Thoroughbred mares, have produced a remarkable record of success, particularly when it is realised that the annual number of foals bred by these stallions is no more than 2000. Some 10,000 Hannoverians are bred each year with a far less successful result. By the HIS scheme (Hunters' Improvement Society, the secondary title of the NLHBS) numerous eventers are

Current Magic, champion at the National Light Horse Breeding Society's annual show for Thoroughbred stallions

bred, including a regular succession of Badminton winners. We have our share of showjumpers, and plenty of point-to-pointers and winners over fences, including a Grand National horse and numerous winners of the principal jumping races.

More importantly the scheme produces what might be termed a sound, crosscountry horse or hunter. The sort of all-rounder which most of us want, since a 'hunter' should be able to take part in a variety of pursuits.

In general, however, Britain does not seem to produce a lot of home-grown dressage horses of note. But that is more likely to be the fault of our training and riding (or possibly the variety of our interests) than of our horses. Those looking to buy a dressage horse are, as a result, more likely to look at a promising warm-blood prospect. Apart from that, the Continental horses have much to offer and are increasingly available at what, in general, are sensible prices.

Probably the best-known in Britain are the Hannoverian, the Dutch Warm-Blood, and, to only a slightly lesser degree, the Trakehner. There are also the Holstein, Oldenburg, Danish and Swedish Warm-Bloods, as well as the tough and versatile Selle Française.

The *Hannoverian* is a big, strongly-built horse which has made a name for itself showjumping and in dressage competitions. It has the sort of temperament that allows it to submit without resentment to the rigorous discipline of the manège (unlike so many horses of more Thoroughbred type) and the breed has a particular gymnastic quality. As a crosscountry horse it is not, I believe, the equal of the English or Irish hunter, and its critics will claim that it lacks the necessary boldness and cleverness in that area, as well as the speed needed in modern eventing, for instance.

The *Dutch Warm-Blood* is one of the success stories

of the post-Second World War era. Without doubt it has been promoted skilfully and the fact that the late Caroline Bradley jumped a Dutch entire so successfully, whilst Jennie Loriston-Clarke obtained the first English World Championship bronze in dressage on another Dutch stallion, has focussed attention on the breed. There is, however, no doubt of the value of the Dutch horses in competition nor of the equability of their temperament. A further cross to the Thoroughbred gives the scope and perhaps the all-important spark for a crosscountry performer.

The *Trakehner* is very much the 'class' horse of the warm-bloods, resembling more closely the British ideal, and he is reputed to be better suited to eventing than the others.

A top-class Hannoverian. The breed is particularly suited to showjumping and dressage

Dutch Courage, Jennie Loriston-Clarke's greatest dressage horse, is an excellent example of the Dutch Warm-blood

When a 'British Horse', the equivalent of the Continental warm-blood, finally appears as something like an entity and with a supporting performance record incorporated in its passport, it will, as does our present-day version, rely heavily on Thoroughbred blood, with a background, as I have indicated of Arab, Mountain and Moorland, Cleveland Bay or Irish Draught and perhaps a few will have a touch of heavy-horse blood.

Such horses are available now and so one should pay regard to those, like the *Irish Draught* and *Cleveland Bay,* which have not been discussed previously. Both the Irish Draught, (a *type,* not a breed) which is represented in Britain by its own society, and the Cleveland Bay, the only native British riding and carriage horse, are riding horses in their own right, the latter more so, possibly,

A good specimen of an Irish Draught. The head is possibly a little heavy but this is nonetheless a good sort

A TB/Irish Draught cross in action. Although plain, this mare is a good performer

A Cleveland Bay stallion displaying the substance and bone which are typical of the breed

than the former. They are, however, massive horses, not, perhaps, entirely suitable for other than a very small number of riders. Their great value lies in their use as a cross with the Thoroughbred, a cross which produces a riding horse of size, substance and bone but with a greater quality, more scope and freedom of movement.

Appaloosa
In recent years the popularity of the *Appaloosa* has been on the increase in Europe and particularly in Britain,

which now has its own British Appaloosa Society. The name Appaloosa originates with the Nez Perce Indians whose country once bordered the Palouse River, from whence the name derives. However, spotted horses of this type have been recorded in Europe as long ago as 20,000 years, centuries before the horse, including the spotted variety, was reintroduced into the American Continent, after a period of some 10,000 years, by the Spanish *conquistadores* of the sixteenth century.

A champion Appaloosa who hunts, events, showjumps and does a good dressage test

As a spectacular riding horse the Appaloosa has achieved some success in recent years and it is claimed that this spotted horse has a remarkably equable temperament in addition to its striking colouring.

Other than the specific breeds there are also available those recognisable *types,* about whose ancestry not very much may be known. A great many people buy just this sort of horse. The difference between a breed and a type may be defined thus: a breed, for the moment, is composed of a group of horses or ponies that have been selectively bred over a sufficient period of time to ensure the consistent production of stock that has in common clearly defined characteristics of height, conformation, colour and action. In addition such stock must be the progeny of 'pure-bred' parents whose pedigrees (for three or four generations or more) are recorded in the stud book of the governing breed society. In turn, of course, the progeny are eligible for similar registration.

Types of horses are those that do not qualify as breeds because they lack conformational consistency or fixed characteristics. (Ref. *A Standard Guide to Horse and Pony Breeds,* E. Hartley Edwards 1980.)

Principal amongst these are the *hunter, hack, cob* and *riding horse,* the latter a useful category created for those horses which fit into none of the others. We could also include the polo pony, but that, of course, is a specialised requirement which it is not necessary to discuss here.

Hunter

Essentially, the word 'hunter' must be allowed to describe any animal that goes hunting, whatever its shape, size or colour. There is, therefore, an infinite variety, ranging from the 15.2 hh small hunter up to the 16-17 hh horse capable of carrying 14-15 st across a galloping country. Show hunters exemplify the best type in the various weight and height divisions. Surprisingly, most of them do hunt, or end up hunting.

An almost perfect pattern for nearly every purpose, the champion hunter Dual Gold

However, as I have said previously, any animal that qualifies as a hunter, ie a sound horse with quality, up to the weight required of it and capable of carrying that weight twice a week, safely and expeditiously, over a fenced country, for perhaps as much as five hours under saddle, must be accounted as the sort of horse that will do a bit of showjumping, compete in dressage tests to medium standard, go team-chasing or eventing (up to intermediate level) and generally be an all-round performer.

Conformation, or the correctness of the make and shape, is obviously of the greatest importance in such a horse and soundness is of paramount consideration, but appearance is less important. Handsome is as handsome does, and a plain head or a goose-rump are neither here nor there unless it is the intention to exhibit the horse in the show ring, where a different set of criteria is applied. Some of the best hunters are those bred in Ireland. They have an uncanny cat-like cleverness about them, are usually bold (if not beautiful) and they have a highly developed sense of self-preservation.

Hack

A hack, if it is considered in terms of the show ring, is usually near-Thoroughbred, although today we see

The very famous show hack, Brown Buzzard, showing great fluency of action

many hacks that are no more than overheight ponies. A hack is, or should be, a horse, albeit the most elegant of horses. It does not require the bone and substance of the hunter, since its powers of endurance are never going to be tested seriously. It does not need to be up to weight, beyond the relatively small amount of *avoirdupois* it is required to carry in the ring, but it must be brimful of personality, straight in its movement, balanced to the nth degree and, in the hands of a competent horseman, well-mannered and entirely obedient without, like your Teutonic product, being absolutely subservient.

Cob

I confess to having a soft spot for the cob as a fun horse that can be put to nearly every equine pursuit. This is the

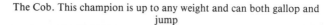

The Cob. This champion is up to any weight and can both gallop and jump

The Welsh Cob cross (usually with a Thoroughbred) is often a very good all-round prospect for the one-horse owner and makes an excellent hunter

gamin, the characterful if well-upholstered urchin of the horse world, full of character and with no little ability.

In essence, the cob, round-bodied on short, strong limbs, is a product of fluke breeding. Most of them come from Ireland, some from South and West Wales and not a few from the West Country, where a group of enthusiastic Highland pony breeders are intent upon breeding a Peninsular Cob, based on Highland, Breton and Thoroughbred blood.

Originally, the cob evolved (accidentally) as a mount for elderly gentlemen. At about 14-15 hh it was easy to mount and it was supposed to have all the attributes of a gentleman's gentleman. Cobs often have a bit of knee action and some may be a shade short in front of the saddle but most are tough customers and an ideal choice for those who want a sensible, not very fast, mount who jumps and is not difficult to keep.

The author's cob Max, a remarkable performer. This picture was taken when Max was over 25 years of age

I have one (see the photograph above) who in a tight country could not be bettered. One might hesitate about sending him into a big spread, but at an upright (up to 6ft) he is unbeatable, having a remarkable gymnastic ability even if he measures a shade under 15 hh. He is a coloured horse, bred, I suspect, behind a tinker's cart in Ireland, but like so many cobs he probably has a touch of Irish Draught and more than a dash of Thoroughbred in his make-up.

My farrier avers that a good coloured horse must be a

tough one, since most are bred by tinkers and gypsies. 'If', he says, 'they can put up with them b——— and survive, then I reckon they'll do very well with the likes of us.'

Riding Horse

I am not so sure about the qualities of a riding horse. Presumably the term should apply to any horse carrying a saddle, but I suspect it is the sort of all-rounder without the elegance of a hack or the conformation of a cob that fails to have the bone, substance and action of a top-class hunter. In fact, the sort of useful, uncomplicated horse which suits a great many people.

A very good stamp of riding horse, suitable for a variety of purposes

Once more I reiterate that the breed or type of horse selected depends upon the purpose for which it is required, the facilities for keeping the animal and the proficiency and ambition of the rider.

3 Where to Buy

As a purchase, it is immaterial whether you go to Tattersall's or Aldridges, to Meynell's Hunt or His Majesty's, it is probable you will be taken in wherever you go.
Geoffrey Gambado (Sir Wm. Bunbury) 1750-1811, *Annals of Horsemanship*

At the outset let me advise you not to take Sir William too seriously, despite the fact that horses are not entirely predictable.

Public Sale
Horses can be bought from a variety of sources, beginning perhaps with the traditional public sale. Most of these are well-established and conducted by highly-reputable firms and some may be concerned with particular breed societies. Increasingly, there is a tendency to hold special sales at centres round the country. Most of the Continental breed societies hold sales in their own countries which give buyers every opportunity to see the horses working and to inspect them closely.

Buyers at sales are as much protected by the law as when making a purchase in any other way. It is as well, however, to study the catalogue carefully, particularly with regard to the auctioneers' ruling regarding the return of unsuitable horses and the general conditions of sale. If a horse does not fulfil the description given in the catalogue or fails in respect of any warranty made there then it can be returned under the conditions laid down by the auctioneers. These conditions are generally uniform but there can be minor differences and for that reason prospective buyers should study the catalogue with care. You cannot, however, return the horse if, having got him home, you don't like his colour or you find that you don't get on with him as well as you thought might be the case.

Sometimes there may be an opportunity for prospective purchasers to arrange to ride a horse prior to it going to auction, but essentially the public sale does not allow the buyer to make the same thorough examination and trial of his purchase as he would be able to do in a private transaction, although there is nothing to prevent his making enquiries about an entry prior to the sale. He has to accept, largely, the description in the catalogue and the evidence provided by his own observation. For that reason, as much as any, auctioneers frame their conditions of sale to ensure, contrary to Geoffrey Gambado's assertion, that buyers will not be 'taken in'.

Mind you, those conditions are made to safeguard the interests of the vendor, also. It would be quite wrong to suppose that it is the purchaser who is always at risk. Very often it is the vendor who needs to be protected from the unscrupulous, or sometimes plain ignorant, buyer. Indeed, in many cases where people buy unsuitable horses, the fault is entirely with them, for they have not taken the trouble to acquire sufficient knowledge to be able to buy so complex a creature as a horse. As we shall see in Chapter 6, relating to the law, the principle is one of *caveat emptor,* let the buyer beware, the law presuming that the purchaser knows something about what he is buying.

When buying at public auction the buyer is relying on his own skill. It is possible for him to buy very satisfactorily and he may, indeed, get a bargain from time to time.

Let me emphasise again that there is no reason to suppose that a horse offered at public auction is other than genuine. In fact, the conditions of sale and the descriptions given are a good deal more binding than the assurances sometimes made in a private deal. Many people when selling horses prefer to send them to a sale rather than to put up with the often time-consuming and time-wasting business of selling privately.

Unsoundnesses of wind which have been subject to an operation, crib-biting and wind-sucking have to be included in the description of any horse to which either one is applicable. Most horses will be sold with a veterinary certificate 'lodged in the office', but, of course, there is nothing to prevent a buyer having the horse vetted again by his own vet as soon as the animal is got home.

The sort of sales to avoid are those held in conjunction with small markets and so on. The auctioneers may not be experienced in selling horses, there are unlikely to be many safeguards and the horses are likely to be a reflection of these circumstances. It is possible to pick up a bargain but you could be buying a lot of trouble also.

The Dealer

For those not sufficiently confident in their ability to buy at public sale, or, indeed, those who just prefer buying in circumstances in which there is a closer relationship between the parties concerned and in which adequate trial and inspection of the horse is offered, the dealer in horses is the solution. It is possible that you may pay a little more, but then you are buying a service as well as a horse, and you have very many in-built safeguards, not the least of which is concerned with the dealer's reputation and good name. There are, of course, dealers and dealers, ranging from the little girl up the road who may run a bit of a riding school to the established, experienced dealer operating a proper business and, like any good businessman, anxious to provide the customer with the goods he requires at a fair price.

Tell a dealer what it is you want, how much you are prepared to pay and allow him a little time to find a horse if there is not one to hand, and he will probably find something suitable. There will be ample opportunity to see the horse ridden and to ride it, and many dealers will arrange to let you have a day's hunting on the animal. If, later on, through no defect of his own, the horse just does not suit you, a dealer will usually find you another and take the first horse back, although, not unreasonably, there may be some cash adjustment.

Most riding schools (and I am thinking of the properly equipped establishments of standing) will have a dealing side to the business, even if it is only a sideline. If one has ridden regularly at the school, there can be advantages in buying a horse from such a source. The proprietor will have a good idea of your ability as a rider and will know the sort of horse that will be the most suitable for you.

Be careful, however, of riding school horses as such. The good old riding school steady, doing plenty of work and used to his regular routine, may behave perfectly in his environment. Away from it, however, he may be quite a different horse and not nearly so manageable. Be careful, too, of the hunt horse, hunted perhaps by the huntsman or whipper-in. He will certainly have done a lot of work in his time but what is even more relevant is that he will have got used to being ridden in front with hounds and may not take kindly to relinquishing his privileged position for the comparative obscurity of being a member of the field and having to take his turn.

The other sorts to be approached with care are the gross, virtually unrideable, fellow out in the field with his shoes off and his feet in need of a trim and, conversely, the horse in very poor condition.

Neither can be tried satisfactorily and both will certainly be quite different horses when got into something like condition. If the make and shape is right, the buyer capable of assessing a horse in these conditions and confident enough in his own ability to put matters in order may have a good buy, for since much must be taken on trust the price has to be commensurate. On the other hand, the less experienced may find themselves landed with the wrong horse.

Buying Privately
By far the greater number of horses are bought from advertisements appearing in the equestrian press. *Horse and Hound* is full of such adverts each week and clearly satisfactory sales are made in this way.

However, it is by no means all plain sailing and it can be an expensive exercise if one drives long distances to view. It is really quite surprising how carried away people can become when describing their horses and how inaccurate are the eulogies which they pen with such enthusiasm. 'Well up to weight' can turn out to be a blood weed able to carry 10-11 st with an effort. One should be wary of all those horses with 'potential' to do this or that. It is not being unkind or condescending to say that the less-experienced vendor (like the less-experienced buyer) can pose something of a problem. It is not for a moment that they seek to misrepresent what they have to sell, but because of their limited knowledge they may incline towards taking an altogether too rosy view.

I have been recommended a three-year-old 'bound to make a top eventer' by a gentleman whose experience of eventing was confined to a sort of mini-hunter trial at local level. I looked at another completely green animal with no more to commend him than, I imagine, an amiable nature, and on enquiring what he had done was rewarded with the disarming answer, 'Well, nothing really, but I am sure he could do great things if you schooled him!' Flattering, but not very helpful when I was looking for a made hunter.

Then there was the man who was advertising what sounded to be a very nice sort, as indeed he may have been. The horse was advertised as 'the best hunter I have ever owned', which was true, but the owner had neglected to say that it was the only one he had ever owned or that, in fact, he had never been hunting on it!

So far as is possible it is probably more prudent, and less expensive, to confine one's search to within a reasonable area of home. The advantage is that one can make local enquiries about the horse and sometimes learn a lot more about the animal than the owner is prepared to reveal.

The vendor, after all, is under no obligation to tell you everything about his horse, whatever the bearing it might have on the character of the animal. He is obliged under the law only to not misrepresent what he has to sell. So it is up to the purchaser to ask the relevant questions and he can best do that if he has some prior knowledge of the horse.

In any case before travelling long distances to see something it is only sensible to make as searching an enquiry as possible over the 'phone, just to make sure that your journey will not be a wasted one.

If you can hear of a horse for sale that can be recommended by friends that, of course, must be worth looking at – so long, that is, as your friends are pretty knowledgeable. Those considering the purchase of a particular breed, an Arab, for instance, or a Welsh Cob or whatever, will find it useful to contact the secretary of the breed society for information about whom to approach.

4   The Mechanics of Buying

*When you are buying a horse, take care not to fall in
love with him, for when this Passion hath once seized
you, you are no longer in a condition to judge his
imperfections.*

Sieur de Solleysel 1617-1680
*The Compleat Horseman
or Perfect Farrier*

In addition to de Solleysel's excellent advice, be warned
also about buying a horse in a hurry. Take your time
about the purchase and don't be stampeded into buying
by either your own impatience or the silver tongue of the
seller. Mistrust, too, the hoary ploy about 'Mr Jones'
who is set on having the horse and is prepared to send his
box down for him this very afternoon unless, of course,
you buy him first. There may be a 'Mr Jones', but it is
unlikely. What is more probable is that the horse will
still be in the same yard next week.

Buying a horse at a sale is one thing, buying one
privately, either from a dealer or from a private person
is another and allows the buyer to make closer enquiries
and to try out his intending purchase. A very good rule,
however, is never to buy a horse (not even from a
bishop) without having with you a friend, preferably not
a relative, who can act, if necessary as an independent
witness to what transpires.

At the outset the intending purchaser should make the
purpose for which he requires the horse quite clear.

Indeed, it is not unreasonable to ask the vendor to provide a form of guarantee that the horse is sound, quiet to ride in all respects and suitable for whatever may be expected of the animal.

The vendor has, of course, the right to decline such an invitation and the buyer must then use his own judgment about what complexion he puts on the refusal.

Even with such a form of guarantee (and it will be just as binding whether it is written or given verbally) a horse should always be bought 'subject to a veterinary certificate' being provided by one's own veterinary surgeon, or, if you are buying some way from home, by an independent vet. Many people selling horses will offer, without in any way seeking to be dishonest, to provide a veterinary certificate supplied by their own vet. I doubt very much that a member of that honourable profession would conceal any relevant failing in a horse but he is being placed in a difficult position. Obviously, he does not wish to lose a client but on the other hand he cannot put his integrity at risk. If such a veterinary certificate is offered, take it politely, but still insist on having the horse inspected thoroughly by your own vet at your own expense.

A very experienced dealer has suggested that as an ultimate blanket question, one should ask: 'Has the horse any tricks or failings which I should know about?'

So far your questions have established the soundness of the animal; his fitness for the purpose intended; his proper behaviour under saddle, which includes traffic worthiness and, as a result of a negative response to that final query, it can be taken that the horse boxes easily, is no trouble to shoe or clip and is not going to savage you every time you enter his box.

To make doubly sure one could ask specifically about matters like boxing, shoeing, clipping etc. Some horses travel very well in a horsebox, entering and leaving the vehicle without trouble, but are less cooperative about entering a trailer.

In these days, one might also enquire about what drugs, if any, have been administered; if so, which and for what purpose. It is also advisable to ask for a record of the worming programme carried out, 'flu vaccinations, tetanus injections and so on and, where applicable, for the 'papers' showing the breeding.

Obviously, if only as a matter of interest, one will also find out as much about the horse's background as possible, what sort of a performance record he has and possibly something about the performance of his parents, if that information is available.

In future years, as the ideal of full registration becomes a reality with horses having a 'passport' recording all the relevant information about them, the position will be much simplified. For the present, however, it is only sensible to learn as much as possible by asking commonsense questions. Do not, however, think that the asking of questions provides cast-iron assurances covering the horse in any eventuality. Of course it does not, and for that matter neither does the law. All that we are doing is to reduce the likelihood of major errors being made and preventing the rare occurrence of downright dishonesty in a transaction.

To risk labouring the point further, it would be naive to think that because it has been made clear to the seller that a horse is required to compete as a showjumper that the buyer has automatic redress when the horse fails to succeed in that sphere. If it could be shown that the horse, prior to its sale, had consistently refused to enter a jumping arena, let alone jump a fence then, clearly, the buyer would have a case. If, however, a normally willing jumper began to develop a decided stop in the hands of its new owner one might presume, and the law would most probably agree, that the fault could lie more with the rider than the horse.

The fact that a horse is sold as a jumper is in no way a guarantee that it will continue to be successful in the sport.

However, to return to the mechanics of the sale. First, I suggest, having absorbed something of the chapter which discusses conformation, the buyer should have the intended purchase brought out for inspection. The horse should be walked and trotted in hand, so that one can see his action and then looked at carefully so that one not only has the opportunity to note any particular deficiency or failing but has a chance to get an overall impression of the horse.

This overall impression is important for it is revealing of the physical character and general outlook of the horse and can also tell us something about his temperament. To see the whole horse it is necessary to stand back and let him 'fill your eye' – and that can't be done if you spend your time examining individual parts of him at a distance of six inches.

Now see the horse tacked up, or, even better, tack him up and handle him in the box yourself, picking up his feet and so on. Take note of the bridle that he wears and if you think it necessary ask questions about the bitting arrangement.

Now let the vendor, or someone appointed by him, ride the horse *before* you get on. There is no point in your risking the possibility of a firework display. Watch the way the horse goes and ask for it to be popped over a small fence. Watch again whether or not the jump is made freely and with a degree of confidence.

When you get up yourself ride the horse away from the area in which he has been shown to you. If he is going to 'nap' he will probably do so then, particularly as he knows he has a new rider aboard.

Put him over a fence and if there is sufficient room set him alight a little by asking him to gallop on. You will then find how easily or otherwise he comes back to you. If you can ride him for a short distance in traffic, do so by all means.

Having gone through all that you should know whether you like the horse or not. If you want to think about it for a week you probably don't like him enough. ('Like' is quite sufficient at this point, you can fall in love with him later if you wish!)

If you are quite certain that you don't like the horse (and there is absolutely no sense buying a horse for whom you can feel no affection) say so there and then, leave a tip for the groom, if there is one, and make your departure. Otherwise, buy him subject to that vet's certificate being satisfactory.

If you are offered the opportunity of a day's hunting, which would not be unreasonable if that was the purpose for which the horse was required, accept with alacrity.

Some people may be prepared to allow you to take the horse on, say, a week's trial. Obviously, such an offer should not be refused, but be very careful about the insurance arrangements.

On the whole, a trial period is not the accepted norm and few professional dealers and only the most trusting (desperate, or unwise) of private vendors will allow one. There are really far too many drawbacks to the practice from the vendor's viewpoint and little to commend it.

As one dealer said: 'If you let them have a horse on trial they spend a week trying to find fault with it rather than appreciating its good points.'

Finally, a word of warning about your treatment of the horse when you get him home.

Remember that he may have had a long, tiring journey and that the change from the surroundings to which he had become accustomed to a new environment and strange people, can cause him to become confused and, temporarily, to experience a loss of security. Dumb the horse may be, in that he does not have the facility of speech, but unfeeling he certainly is not and he is possessed of considerable sensitivity also.

Give him, therefore, a few days in which to settle down before asking anything very much of him. Spend time in his box, handling him, talking to him and generally making friends.

It is probably wiser to keep him in for a few days so that he becomes accustomed to his surroundings, before turning him out in a paddock, if that is your practice. When and if you turn him out, leave his headcollar on, initially, fitting it with a short rope from the back ring to make it easier to catch him up. Whilst he is in the paddock make a point of giving him a small feed without actually trying to catch him or bring him in. He then associates your appearance with food and not necessarily with being caught.

Young horses, particularly, often seek to test the authority of a new owner, which is neither unreasonable nor unnatural. If the settling-in process is hurried they may even resent being asked to leave the yard under saddle, and attempt to return to the stable.

Deal with these little rebellions firmly, by all means, but try to understand the underlying reasons for them and don't blame the horse or the person who sold him to you.

5 The Law and the Horse

Warrantin' an 'oss is highly inconwenient, 'specially when you've reason to know he's a screw ...

R. S. Surtees 1803-1864
*Handley Cross,
or Mr Jorrocks' Hunt*

The basis of law applicable to the sale or purchase of all types of goods, including the horse, is the ancient one of *caveat emptor,* let the buyer beware, for the law presumes that the buyer knows about what he is buying and if, later on, he finds that his purchase is for one reason or another not what he required he must expect to stand whatever loss is involved.

However, the harsh but not unreasonable reality of *caveat emptor* has been mitigated by legislation which seeks, to a degree, to protect the foolish against their own actions, but for all that *caveat emptor* remains supremely relevant. A 'barrack-room lawyer' is one of the most odious of creatures, only equalled in unpleasantness by his like-minded colleague of the stableyard.

The best advice that can be given in the horse-buying context is for both parties to be aware of the general law pertaining to a commercial contract, and thereafter to ensure by their actions that the law never has to be invoked – for there will be little benefit in that to either party.

In essence there is no reason why the law should loom

larger when it comes to the sale of a horse than for any other commodity. There are, however, some aspects which are worth bearing in mind whether one buys or sells.

Conditions and Warranties

There is, for instance, the law relating to warranties and conditions, and there is a difference in the outcome should there be a breach of either one.

Breach of a condition may entitle the buyer to cancel the contract and to claim a full refund plus expenses. Breach of warranty, which is more common, only allows the claimant to press for damages. In other words if a horse is bought conditionally, eg subject to a *condition* that it was quiet to box, shoe and clip and then subsequently kicked the farrier out of his box persistently, thus making it impossible for the latter to carry out his work, then the breach of condition involved entitles the purchaser to return the horse, get his money back and claim for any costs involved. It can, as may be imagined, become more complicated than that, but in most instances relating to horses we are concerned with *warranties* rather than conditions.

A warranty is best defined in the form given in the *Oxford English Dictionary:* 'An undertaking, express or implied, given by one of the parties to a contract to the other, that he will be answerable for the truth of some statement incidental to the contract; especially an assurance given by the seller of the goods that he will be answerable for their possession of some quality attributed to them.' Or, one might add, 'is free from defects which are warranted against'.

In fact a warranty applies as of the time of the sale, so it is advisable always to buy subject to the horse being given a veterinary certificate, stipulating that this will be provided by one's own vet. So far as the seller is concerned he will still be liable under the warranty if he warrants a horse sound when it possesses a fault, even if at the time he was unaware of that fault. He can, however, safeguard himself by incorporating the words, 'so far as I am aware'.

At public sales particular terms carry more or less specific guarantees. 'Good Hunter', for instance, is a complete warranty that the horse is sound in every respect, is quiet to ride and is capable of being hunted. A 'hunter' has to be quiet to ride and capable of being hunted and he must be sound in wind and eye – which says, far less warrants, nothing so far as the soundness of his action goes.

The words 'believed sound' constitute a warranty of soundness in all respects, whilst 'good performer' is nearly as good as describing a horse as a good hunter but it only admits to the horse being sound at the time of sale and there is no assurance that this has always been the case or that it is likely to be so as far as can be predicted.

Any attribute can be the subject of a warranty but there is no obligation for a vendor to give any warranty at all. Indeed, by the time one has ploughed through the laws relative to the subject one might well wonder why anybody should consider warranting so unpredictable a creature as a horse.

The law, in its wisdom, however, makes provision for the circumstance in which a vendor declines to give a warranty through the Sale of Goods Act 1893 and its amendment by the Supply of Goods (Implied Terms) Act 1973.

Two very relevant sections are section 14 of the 1893 Act amended by section 3 of the 1973 Act, and these are of particular relevance to the sale of horses. They read as follows:

14 (2) 'Where the seller sells goods in the course of a

business, there is an implied condition that the goods supplied under the contract are of merchantable quality, except that there is no such condition: a) as regards defects specifically drawn to the buyer's attention before the contract is made; or b) if the buyer examines the goods before the contract is made, as regards defects which the examination ought to reveal.

(3) 'Where the seller sells goods in the course of a business and the buyer, expressly or by implication, makes known to the seller any particular purpose for which the goods are bought, there is an implied condition that the goods supplied under the contract are reasonably fit for that purpose, whether or not that is a purpose for which such goods are commonly supplied, except where the circumstances show that the buyer does not rely, or that it is unreasonable for him to rely, on the seller's skill and judgment.'

There is a number of points to be noted here. The first is that the sale has to be 'in the course of a business', so whilst it can relate to a dealer whose business is concerned with the sale of horses it is not applicable to a sale between private persons, unless the parties stipulate their inclusion in any contract which is drawn up.

The second very relevant point is contained in (3). John Weatherill *(Horses and the Law,* Pelham Horsemaster Series) gives as an example the instance of a parent telling a dealer that he wanted a child's riding pony and the dealer selling him an unmanageable animal. The parent would then be in a position 'to repudiate the contract on the grounds of a breach of the implied condition'.

As if to prove that the law can sometimes seem to be an ass, the same would apply even if the dealer knew the pony to be unsuitable and advised accordingly, but the client insisted upon buying the animal.

The dealer would then be well-advised to obtain a waiver from his client which admitted that the pony was being bought without reliance on the dealer's skill and judgment.

Trade Description Act and Misrepresentation

Contravention of the Trade Description Acts 1968-72 can result in criminal charges against anyone who in the course of business offers goods for sale to which a false description is applied. You must not sell a 20-year-old horse as a five-year-old, or claim that some old plod is a Grade A showjumper when he has difficulty negotiating a cavalletto. Or, at least, you must not do so knowingly and in those two instances you could hardly not know that you were bending the truth a trifle.

Again, however, the Act does not apply to the private transaction, although there one could have recourse to a civil claim on the grounds of misrepresentation which could lead to a termination of the contract or a right to claim damages.

Veterinary Certificates

A certificate given by a vet although no more than the expression of a professional opinion by a suitably qualified person is, in a sense, a partial guarantee, for if the vet is horribly negligent or does not exercise the standard of skill normally expected of his profession he lays himself open to a claim being made against him.

Essentially, the normal form of certificate is one which states that the vet has examined the animal in question in accordance with a laid-down standard practice and finds no clinical signs of disease, injury or physical abnormality which would affect its use for the purpose which his client states the horse is required.

More than that you cannot ask or expect.

By all means let the buyer beware, but the dealer, the vet and even the private person needs also to beware, for the law embraces all.

6 Applied Conformation

*What a piece of work is a horse! How noble in reason!
How infinite in faculty! In form and moving how
express and admirable! In action how like an angel! In
apprehension how like a man! The beauty of the world!
The paragon of animals!*

> James Agate (1877-1947)
> *Alarums and Excursions*

Conformation has to be a considerable consideration in
the purchase of a horse, for so much is dependent upon
the physical shape. The performance, or the potential
performance, is most certainly closely related to the
horse's conformation in terms of movement, balance
and athletic quality. Additionally, and it is not always
fully appreciated, conformation can be a governing
factor in the temperament of the individual.

Therefore, it behoves the prudent purchaser to have
some knowledge of good and bad conformation,
enough certainly to be able to recognise the salient
points of both conditions, as well as having an overall
appreciation of the importance of buying well-made
horses and an understanding of the differences in make
and shape which cause one horse to be more suitable for
a particular pursuit than another.

Everyone, I imagine, has a general understanding of
the word 'conformation', as relating to the shape or
form of the horse, but it is perhaps worth reminding
ourselves of the excellent definitions provided by the

Oxford English Dictionary. They are these: 'the forming or fashioning of a thing in all its parts' and 'form depending upon arrangement of parts; structure'.

When applied specifically to the horse the definition will benefit, perhaps, from some enlargement.

In effect, we are talking about the formation of the skeletal frame (the foundation, as it were) and its accompanying muscle structures in terms of the symmetrical proportion to each other of the individual parts comprising the whole.

The key words in these definitions are 'parts' and 'proportion'. In the end it is the perfection of each component and their proportionate relationship which contributes to the perfection of the overall form. In the well-made horse no one feature disturbs the general symmetry by being unduly accentuated or by being insufficiently so.

Exactly what constitutes a 'proportional' horse is rather more difficult to define, but the mechanical efficiency of equine proportion has been the subject of scientific study. Probably the best-known conclusions are those of Professor Wortley Axe who based his measurements on the calculations of Bourgelat and Dulrousset.

Overleaf is a diagram of Wortley Axe's efficiently 'proportioned' horse (Fig. 2) and there is no doubt that it provides useful guidelines which are generally applicable.

Basic conformation, in terms of the correct and harmonious proportion and placement of the component parts and the proper formation of the latter, is common to all equines. But the proportions, while combining to produce a symmetrical shape overall, will vary according to the purpose for which the horse is required. As a further rider to the basic definitions we can, therefore, say that the desirable conformation in

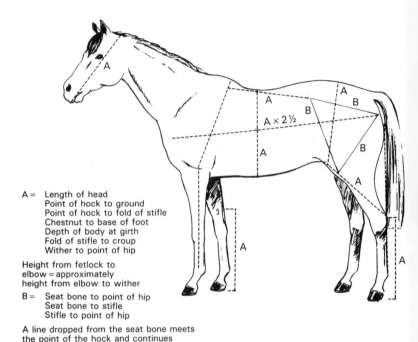

A = Length of head
Point of hock to ground
Point of hock to fold of stifle
Chestnut to base of foot
Depth of body at girth
Fold of stifle to croup
Wither to point of hip

Height from fetlock to
elbow = approximately
height from elbow to wither

B = Seat bone to point of hip
Seat bone to stifle
Stifle to point of hip

A line dropped from the seat bone meets
the point of the hock and continues
down the back of the cannon bone

Fig. 2 Wortley Axe's efficiently proportioned horse

any horse is concerned with a framework, the construction of which, in terms of the proportion, shape and placement of the individual parts, is relative to the required purpose.

In brief the sort of desirable conformation in a draught horse, which is required to draw heavy loads at a slow pace, will virtually be the opposite to that of the racehorse where the overriding criterion is speed.

In between those extremes will be found variations imposed either by natural environment, selective breeding, often to a particular end, or, of course, by a combination of both.

In the first instance there is the example of the British

native pony whose background of rough mountain and moorland terrain has resulted in a characteristic way of moving which is dependent upon the critical shape and placement in the shoulder of the scapula in relation to the humerus. Because of this arrangement, which may appear to give somewhat less slope to the shoulder, the ponies move with some action from the knee. That means that although it is the shoulder that initiates the movement and governs the length of stride taken, the knee is bent to give a higher action. A well-made native pony raises the foreleg and then stretches it forward to the limit of its extension before putting it down. The action is therefore both economical and ground covering (ie the leg is not just lifted up and put down with only a minimum of ground being covered with each stride). It is because of this environmentally evolved action that ponies, like the Welsh, can cross rough ground expeditiously and safely without stumbling or falling over rocks, gulleys, tussocks etc, and it is thus entirely suited to their purpose.

The show pony, an artificial product in comparison, though infinitely beautiful, and the result of the most skilful selective breeding, moves the foreleg from the shoulder, pointing the toe in a near 'daisy-cutting' action which involves minimum flexion of the knee joint. The stride may positively devour the ground and the comfort of the ride is indisputable but only so long as one is talking about relatively level going. On the really rough mountain terrain such an action would be a positive disadvantage – but then the show pony does not have to survive on a mountain and was not bred for that purpose.

The American Quarter Horse is an example of selective breeding with a particular purpose in view. Not only was the Quarter Horse indispensable for working cattle, developing an innate ability to anticipate the quick movements and to stop and turn at breakneck speed, largely on account of his strongly developed quarters, but he was also the racehorse of the early settlers. Having no proper facilities racing was often a matter of a short sprint down the dust-track village street or in some suitable clearing. The breed took its name from these races which were usually over a distance of about a quarter mile. To excel over such a distance the Quarter Horse needed to accelerate to maximum speed from the standing start in a matter of a stride or two. To do so he needed enormous power in his quarters and at one point in the breed's development breeders were producing animals so muscle-bound in this department that they appeared to be almost disproportionate in the overall outline.

The final factor in the assessment of conformation rests with the criteria applied by the human agency, and this, obviously, varies according to the background and experience of the observer. It might, indeed, be said that conformation is in the eye of the beholder.

The Continental horseman who because of climatic conditions and possibly lack of opportunity to ride across open country looks for the conformation (and, of course, the temperament) suited to the activities available to him, much of which may be concerned with indoor riding involving dressage and jumping. A horse's ability to gallop is therefore not relevant to his needs and the sort of conformation that fits a horse to gallop would not come within his experience. His ideal is the strong powerful horse, a shade heavy in comparison to one of more Thoroughbred type, of shorter proportions and with a very much more phlegmatic nature. Such a horse besides being powerful enough for jumping, particularly over big, puissance-type courses, will also be suited to the dressage discipline, where speed is of no consequence, and will have, as it were, the ability to 'sit down on his bottom', which is one of the criteria I would personally apply in this context. If you prefer, it is the broadly-based horse that is needed; a conformation not so often found in the Thoroughbred sort, who is longer and narrower.

In Britain, as, of course, in Ireland and America, as well as in France, where selective breeding of Thoroughbred/Anglo-Arab competition horses has been practised extensively and over a long period, the horseman, conditioned by a background of outdoor riding (hunting, racing and so on) looks for a different sort. He needs the galloping horse of scope and, above all, courage, and the indoor horse is just not suited to his requirement.

It is argued that in Britain, for instance, we do not breed horses suitable for dressage (or at least that is the argument of those who have embraced the Continental Warm-Blood). I am not sure that is the case. It is true that what are generally more highly-couraged horses are not so submissive to school discipline as the commoner horse, many of the Continentals having that background of equable coaching blood. On the other hand we do have horses whose temperament would be suitable for the purpose. What we may not have are enough riders of a similar nature who are prepared, and capable, of training a dressage horse in a logical sequence from the age of three.

As a final example of what may be entirely acceptable to one man and anathema to another, there is the Andalusian of Spain and Portugal, once the first horse in all Europe and the noble ancestor of the Lipizzaner. He does, indeed, have a noble bearing, 'fit to carry a King on the day of his triumph', but his rolling, extravagantly round and uneconomic dishing action (where the foreleg is lifted and carried outwards in a half-circle before being returned to the ground) would be condemned out-of-hand in an English show ring as it would be for most competitive purposes. On the other hand, a flamboyant action of this sort is much esteemed in his own country where the Andalusian is, incidentally, the traditional mount of the *rejoneadore,* the mounted bullfighter. He is, of course, no great galloper, although the fairly recent introduction of Thoroughbred blood will improve him in that respect, but he is extraordinarily agile and athletic and undeniably showy!

A Spanish Andalusian in the long reins. The breed is very powerful in the quarters but not built for great speed

Similarly, the Lipizzaner of the sort used at the Spanish Riding School is no great example of equine

perfection. Indeed, his inability to extend ensures that he has little or no success in international dressage competition and otherwise there are few pursuits he could follow which would not be better accomplished by a dozen other breeds and types. Nonetheless, he reigns supreme within the confines of his own setting, and who would ask for more than that?

Possible Effects of Conformation
Essentially, a horse of good conformation should have a longer working life than one of bad conformation, for the reason that being more mechanically efficient he has that much more chance of standing up to work and remaining sound.

Any deficiency in conformation, anything which is out of accord with the overall symmetry, is a potential weakness, and when the horse is placed in circumstances of physical stress this is the area which will be the first to give way. Let us say that a horse has a 'twisted foreleg', one that is a little out-of-true and not a match with its partner. Because of such a deficiency – which is not by any means unusual – the natural strains and stresses imposed in active movement, when the horse is, additionally, carrying weight, will be concentrated on one part of a joint, for instance, instead of over the whole of the bearing surface. Also, ligaments may be subjected to uneven strains and it is probable that diseases of the foot, caused by it being out of true and therefore subjecting the parts to unequal wear, will become apparent.

Weak, cow hocks will result in more uneven strains producing curbs, thoropins or spavins. A horse with dropped soles (flat feet, if you like) is more likely to suffer damage on rough going than otherwise. Those with unduly long backs, which amounts to a serious structural weakness, as well as those with very short ones will be more disposed to back troubles. One could continue indefinitely in this vein.

PERFORMANCE

All else being equal good conformation should result in comparable performance levels. It may not always do so since we are not, despite all our measurements and mechanical theories, dealing with a machine. The successful competition horse, or just a plain good hunter, is what he is because of his willingness to cooperate with the human requirement, which must often be both unnatural and even incomprehensible to him. Without that mental alignment the most perfectly proportioned horse may be a disaster in terms of performance. However, one does have the opportunity of making some assessment of an animal's performance capacity before one gets to the point of buying him.

Conversely, of course, a few horses with what appear to be notable conformational deficiencies are brilliant performers, possibly because they have some sort of highly-developed competitive instinct. Most of them, however, if examined carefully will be seen to have a compensating physical factor which goes some way to making up for the defect. On the whole, however, badly made horses are poor performers and bad buys.

Performance, of course, is also a matter of training, and in schooling the horse a prime consideration is the logical development of his physique. In pursuit of that end it is necessary to make the horse supple laterally and longitudinally and, in particular, perhaps, to strengthen and supple the hindlegs equally. It is far more difficult, if not impossible, to develop a badly made horse so that he uses his limbs and body force with equal effect. In fact, the horse with physical irregularities may be forced into becoming uneven in his paces and compelled to make compensatory resistances. But more of that when we come to consider the effect of conformation on the all-important temperament.

BALANCE

What is certain, is that the well-made horse is a well-balanced horse. Good balance in a horse contributes to an athletic, even gymnastic, capability, and thus to better performance with less risk of physical strain. It facilitates schooling and it is, of course, so much more comfortable for the rider, since the horse is virtually carrying himself. Furthermore, the balanced horse is more easily positioned and controlled. He is always, because of his state of balance, in a position which allows him to go forward freely from the leg and, conversely, to come back easily to the hand.

ACTION

Movement, or action, is a direct result of conformation. Straight, properly formed limbs in the mature horse, combined with the other desirable attributes, result in free, straight and elastic action. The stride is not shortened by a misplacement of the forearm, or by a straight and loaded shoulder. Less effort is therefore expended, there is less risk of the horse striking into himself because he goes too close in front or behind, and therefore less risk of injury leading to possible unsoundness.

TEMPERAMENT

An all-important consideration in the horse is that of temperament, which in my view is formed largely, but not entirely, by the sort of contact he has with human beings. Obviously, every horse has a nature of his own but the way in which it is developed is very much dependent upon the human.

There is a saying that 'all horses are fit for Heaven, whilst only a few men are'. That I believe may be so, for I am convinced of the truth of yet another old tag: 'No horse was born evil but man made him so.' And, if you want another for good measure: 'There are no problem horses, only problem people.'

That a horse's conformation has an effect upon his temperament is not really accurate, because it ignores the principal villain, the human. What we should say (with some humility) is that as a result of our inability or unwillingness to recognise the limitations imposed on the horse by conformational weaknesses or irregularities there may be adverse effects on his temperament.

If the horse is compelled to perform exercises or do work which because of some physical weakness makes him uncomfortable or even cause pain, then he will make some resistance as the only way of telling his rider/trainer of the irritation. If the human persists, as most humans do, the discomfort increases and the horse becomes sour and resentful – then he becomes a problem horse.

Temperamental difficulties are frequently caused by horses being forced into a particular carriage when their physical conformation makes it impossible for them to adopt such an outline without their experiencing discomfort. Horses that because of the way in which the head joins the neck have difficulty in flexing from the poll are just such an example. In their case the use of draw reins, or other artificial devices designed to force the head into the desired position, becomes a positive cruelty.

This, of course, is the trouble with so many of the

'training aids', or 'gadgets' as they are often called. In themselves and used judiciously by very experienced people they are as legitimate as the active leg and the intermittently restraining hand that causes the horse to shorten his outline. The trouble is that they can be used injudiciously by the inexperienced and if the horse has difficulty in complying with the demands made, because his conformation does not allow him to do so without his being made uncomfortable, they become instruments of coercion which in the end destroy the horse's trust and confidence and make him sullen and unwilling.

Details of Conformation

The extremes of conformation are exemplified by the draught horse on the one hand and the Thoroughbred horse on the other. Length in the proportions and the muscle formation of the latter produce speed whilst the opposite conformation of the Shire, for instance, is indicative of physical strength and power at, of course, slow paces. In between we have horses more or less inclined to speed or more or less inclined to strength.

When assessing conformation visually one needs first to stand off and view the whole horse. He should, we are told, 'fill the eye' and that is not a bad description, for if the overall outline is noticeably asymmetrical or there is some notable deficiency the horse will neither 'fill' nor please the eye. However, it is necessary in any study of conformation to examine the components forming the structure in some detail and what better place to begin than with the *head,* a part of the horse which, as in the human being, can reveal much of the character and, in the case of the horse, the antecedents too.

HEAD
Lean, finely chiselled heads with the bone formation

lightly covered with skin are indications of breeding and are usually to be found in Thoroughbred and Arab horses and their near-derivatives.

The profile in the well-bred horse is either straight or slightly concave, but in the Arabian there is a very definite 'dish' to the front line of the face and this characteristic feature frequently appears in more or less accentuated form in horses carrying a percentage of Arab blood.

The dish face of the Arab, almost always accompanied by the wide flaring nostril, is much prized by Arabian enthusiasts, but in recent years at least one authority has suggested that breeders may have gone too far in this respect and could be restricting the free passage of air as a result. Whether that is so or not is by the by but it is interesting to note the degree of refinement which can be achieved by the selective breeding of pure-bred stock.

Pictures of the early Crabbet Arabians, imported to Britain from Arabia by Wilfrid and Anne Blunt at the end of the nineteenth century, often show horses which by present-day standards would be considered very plain in the head. Captain Horace Hayes, the eminent veterinarian who published his *Points of the Horse* in 1893, included photographs of 'high-caste Arabs' which would be virtually unrecognisable as such today because of the almost complete absence of what we now think of as the 'characteristic' dish face.

The term 'dry' is frequently used when referring to the Arab horse. This dry look comes because of the very thin skin-covering on the head which allows the veins to be clearly traced. Refinement in the head, whatever the breed, creates an immediate impression of interest and alertness and such horses will have a greater sensitivity and be more responsive and swift in their reactions than animals of more plebeian ancestry. (They may, indeed, be altogether too quick and too highly couraged for other than the most competent riders.)

The less highly bred horse, possibly with some heavy horse or other cold-blood type in his background, can be expected to have a heavier appearance about the head in varying degrees. The hair covering the head is thicker and wiry to the touch and the skin itself is not so thin. A light covering of hair which, in the Arab for instance, is silky in texture, is a prerogative of the well-bred horse.

A very heavy 'carty' sort of head is usually associated with lethargy and slow reactions. A Roman nose, giving a marked convex profile, derives from the heavy horse and many weight-carriers betray the outcross in their ancestry by exhibiting this particular feature. In fact, on a big hunter a Roman nose gives, in my view, a pleasant, homely and honest look to the head. Certainly, many horsemen hold the Roman nose in some regard, although very few will approve of a horse with a pronounced bump between the eyes. In these cases the eyes are often small and piggy and thus to be avoided as a sign of an ungenerous spirit. From a practical viewpoint it is desirable for the bone at the top of the head (the occipital crest) to be prominent, as it is the attachment-point for the suspensory ligament of the head and neck.

Of all the parts of the head the *eye* is the most revealing of character but its placement is also worthy of consideration. Later in this chapter the question of vision in the horse is discussed in more detail but for the moment it will suffice to say that the eyes in a riding horse need to be placed as much to the front of the head as possible, which means that the forehead itself cannot be too broad, although, obviously, it should not be exaggeratedly narrow. In the riding horse, which is expected to gallop and jump, forward vision is necessary and horses for this purpose whose eye placement inclines too much towards pronounced lateral vision are best avoided. In the heavy breeds the eyes are placed to the side of the head which improves the animal's lateral vision but, of course, at the expense of frontal sight.

Large, generous eyes, give a kind expression to the face and are nearly always indicative of a corresponding nature. I am not too happy about horses that show the white of their eyes, they make me apprehensive. Often it is no more than a natural pigmentation; the Appaloosa, for instance, has a white sclera to the eye which is characteristic of the breed, one that has a reputation for being good-tempered and amenable. However, there are horses who show the white of the eye with evil intent, accompanying the action with laid-back ears and dilated nostrils. I am told that such horses, as well as being generally unpleasant characters, have a remarkable ability as cow-kickers as well.

The question then arises as to whether this temperamental failing is inherited or whether it comes about because of the horse's experience with Man. If it is inherited, was it first implanted by the human? Take your choice. Don't blame the horse too much – but don't buy him either.

Wall eyes, sometimes found in cream and part-coloured horses are unsightly, perhaps, but they are not detrimental to performance and not indicative of any ill-will. They occur only because of a lack of pigment in the iris. Distinct hollows above the eyes (the *supra-orbital fossa*) are usually an indication of age but horses in very fit condition may also have slight hollows, since there will be an absence of superfluous fat. Similarly, the progeny of an old dam may exhibit this peculiarity.

The essential triumvirate in any study of the head, or indeed of the horse as a whole, is that comprising eyes, ears and nostrils. They provide us with a remarkable sum of information. The *ears* are, for me, objects of great importance. It is through them that we are able to have a clear visual indication of our horse's state of mind whilst we are in the saddle. I like ears to be thinly covered with skin, very mobile and easily pricked. Most books will say that they should be small and neat but I do not object if they are large, so long as they fulfil the remaining criteria. Ears, in a sense, supplement the horse's vision, for he makes much use of his hearing. They can, of course, be too long, too heavy and move too sluggishly and are then indicative of a phlegmatic character who will be slow in his responses and reactions.

Lop ears, which are carried out sideways, are, of course, heavy ears. They have a certain visual appeal and lop-eared horses are reputed to be very genuine sorts. There is, however, a disadvantage. The ears are carried thus because of some loss of nerve control but their lack of movement gives the rider no clue as to the intentions of his horse.

Since the horse breathes solely through the nose and has large lung cavities to fill with air, the *nostrils* should be large and wide so that there can be a maximum inhalation of air when the animal is working at speed. Small nostrils are useless to a riding horse.

The lower *jaw* branches need to be widely spaced to allow room for the larynx and also, very importantly, to allow the horse to flex at the poll. Ideally, it should be possible to place a clenched fist between the branches of the jaw.

A *parrot mouth,* where the top jaw overlaps the lower one, or the converse over-shot lower jaw, are both formations which give rise to bitting problems and cause the horse difficulty in grazing.

The size of the head is also a matter of importance, since it is the head, used in conjunction with the neck whch acts as the balancing agent for the body mass. It can be likened to a 40lb (18kg) blob at the end of the pendulum which is the neck. In the simplest terms the horse transfers his weight to the rear by raising his head and neck and shifts it over the forehand by lowering them. In schooling the horse the ability to place the weight over engaged quarters with a heightened carriage of head and neck is critical and it will become almost impossible to accomplish if the size of the head is disproportionate in relation to the neck.

A heavy head on a weak, narrow neck will cause the weight to be carried over the forehand (and on the rider's hand too) and will prohibit attempts to impose a balance based on the quarters. A tiny head, which is far less common, would also act against a proper balance.

Nonetheless a relatively large head set on a comparatively short strong *neck* is acceptable enough in a weight-carrier, so long as all else is in proportion. Such a structure is associated with strength but also, of course, with slower paces. The opposite, lean heads on fairly long graceful necks, are attributes of speed. For the all-round horse, particularly where endurance is a consideration, a light head with a strongly built neck, moderately short in length, is probably the most satisfactory combination.

A number of the stronger built Continental Warm-Bloods have short muscular necks together with heavyish heads. It is certainly not detrimental to their jumping ability nor to their suitability as dressage horses. Theirs is an example of conformation tending slightly more towards the structural strength of the draught horse and away from the long elegance of the Thoroughbred. Such horses may not, of course, have sufficient speed for crosscountry competition. Usually, however, the neck is very flexible and the juncture between head and neck is good enough to enable the poll to be carried high. A high poll carriage with the nose tucked in to a near overbent position is acceptable in a jumper because it is from this viewpoint that he sees a fence most easily.

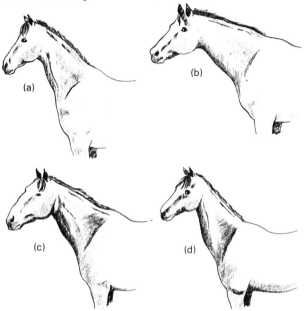

(a) neck too short, good hunter head, neck runs into good shoulder

(b) well set-on neck running into straight shoulder to give a misleading overall impression. Good head

(c) Common head, pig eye, thick nostrils, large jaw bones, pronounced parotid gland. Neck almost upside-down, straight loaded shoulder

(d) ewe neck, straight shoulder, round ribs under saddle, tied-in elbow

Fig. 3 The head and neck

NECK

Just how long the neck should be in a riding horse is dependent upon too many factors to be stated definitively. After all there is the head to be considered as well as all the variations in shape. However, the standard which commands general acceptance is for the neck, from the poll to the highest part of the wither, to be equal to one and a half times the length of the head measured from the poll to the lowest part of the upper lip. It doesn't work with stallions because of their usually crested necks but it is otherwise a not unreasonable guide.

What is important is that the muscles of the neck should be in proportion to those of the foreleg, because it is the former that activate the latter by drawing it forward. Thus in a racehorse, which will usually have a long forearm, the neck has to be of a corresponding length. In the draught horse the forearm is much shorter and so the neck also needs to be short, thick and powerful.

Look, too, at each end of the neck, how at one end it is connected to the head (the setting-on of head to neck), and at the other how it is merged into the shoulder.

An abrupt junction between head and neck which results in a thick, fleshy throat is a bad fault because it will interfere with respiration. Usually this sort of junction is found in horses with extra short, thick necks which may then run into thick upright shoulders. 'Cock-throttled' is the term used to describe horses in whom the angle of head and neck is over-acute. There is excessive length from the base of the ear to the throat and always a bulging parotid gland. As a result of this conformation the larynx is compressed and the breathing restricted seriously.

At the opposite end the neck, which must always be longer on the top side than the lower, should streamline into the shoulders in a graceful, uninterrupted curve. This, however, can only be obtained if the lower end of the neck is sufficiently wide, which means that the neck bones have to be well-formed and the mastoido-humeralis muscle at the junction of neck and shoulder strongly developed.

If the neck seems to end before it reaches the withers, interrupting the smooth curvature, it is a bad conformational fault. In such cases the shoulders when viewed from the front are too wide and the scapula is almost invariably upright instead of sloped. The result of conformation of this sort is a horribly rolling action in front which is not only uneconomical and inefficient but is also very uncomfortable. In the case of the draught horse, however, the riding horse's graceful streamlined juncture of neck and shoulder would be of no consequence and, indeed, detrimental to the animal's purpose. The sloped shoulder, allowing length of stride in the riding horse, would give no support at all to a collar and in a draught horse wide shoulders and big muscles covering the scapula are essential and will prevent pressure on the trachea when the horse is in draught.

So much weight in front is impossible to contemplate in the riding horse but it is very necessary for the draught horse who has to put weight into his collar so as to get his load under way.

The two sorts of neck structure which should be avoided in the riding horse are the ewe-neck and the swan-neck. The former is one in which the top-line is concave, the lower line bulging outwards very objectionably. Bridling problems are almost inevitable with a ewe-neck. In some instances, however, the accentuated muscle formation on the lower side of the neck has been caused by bad riding (of a sort which can be imagined) and some sensible remedial schooling aimed at getting the horse to extend and lower his head and neck, with his nose being the leading point in the progression, will go a long way towards correcting the fault.

Swan-necks are just as bad and though some authorities claim that a horse with this defect can see well and may as a result be a good jumper it is not a fault to be overlooked, nor would one advise the purchase of a swan-necked horse.

A swan-neck is one which is convex in its upper third, the head seeming to have been dropped on vertically and as a result being carried near to the horizontal plane. Once more, it will be difficult to avoid bitting problems and it is almost certain, as with the ewe-necked horse, that trouble will be experienced with the fitting of the saddle, the horse's shape encouraging the latter to slide forward so that the girth rubs hard up against the elbows. Galling will be inevitable and any sort of correct riding technique made impossible to accomplish.

Hackney horses and breeds like the American Saddle-bred are extreme examples of necks being joined to shoulders in something near to the vertical line. Such a conformation gives these breeds their necessarily high and upright carriage of head and neck and the resultant high-stepping action of the forelegs. However, this type of conformation, or even something approaching it, is not a desirable feature in a general riding horse who has no need for that sort of movement, the required action being longer and closer to the ground.

WITHERS

The withers arise from the superior spines of the third to ninth dorsal vertebrae and provide the point of attachment for the muscles which support the forehand and govern its movement. To them are attached the suspensory ligament of the head and neck; the muscles by which the latter is extended and contracted; the muscles of the back; and the muscles which activate the ribs in the inspiration of air and those which attach the shoulder blade (scapula) to the body. Their shape and definition is, therefore, of great import in every type of horse.

A high wither (without it being too exaggerated) is the

most effective in activating, through its attachments, the parts of the forehand and the further its placement to the rear the greater will be the obliquity of the scapula and, in consequence, the greater and more free will be the length of the stride and the more comfortable the ride. A good wither definition well-covered in muscle helps to position the saddle properly and keep it in place, whereas a low, or flat, wither will create fitting problems.

Low, ill-defined withers are usually accompanied by upright shoulders, which, of course, restrict the length of stride materially, producing a choppy, up-and-down action in front which is uneconomical, tiring to both horse and rider and produces greater and more damaging concussion in the lower limbs. Frequently, upright shoulders will be lumpy in appearance because of their being overloaded with muscle and they cause a rolling type of movement in the forehand.

Ponies are rather more disposed to being flat over the withers than horses and some Arabs have a similar conformation. Usually a flat-withered Arab will also have the expected upright shoulder but this is not always so. But then the Arab is something of a law unto himself, as befits his position as the fountain head of the light horse breeds. He rarely, if indeed ever, has the sort of defined wither to be found in the Thoroughbred, but that does not mean he lacks a sloped riding shoulder or a front, it is just that because he is Arab he is different. What is certain is that most common and just about all scrub-bred stock are low and coarse about the wither.

In youngstock it is natural for the croup to be higher than the wither until they reach maturity, but such a situation in an older horse is not to be tolerated – not, that is, if one has regard for the balance, the wear on the forelegs and the comfort of the rider. From those viewpoints wither and croup should be in line, or, ideally, the former should be a little higher. On the other hand the opposite structure may be conducive to greater speed. A draught horse, however, needs to be higher in the wither than the croup if he is to be able to apply effective traction.

SHOULDER

Inevitably, in the preceding pages reference has been made continually to the shoulder and its desirable slope. It is, indeed, a matter of much concern amongst horsemen and a never failing subject of conversation, almost on a par with the weather, in horsey circles.

Almost to the exclusion of everything else, the horse's action, good or bad, depends upon the shape and position of the shoulder blades, which are referred to here as the scapulas. In the riding horse, but not the draught, they need to be close together at the top. If they are wide apart one gets the rolling action and lumpy 'loaded' appearance which has already been mentioned. The tops need to be well sloped to the rear, well 'laid-back', and the blades themselves must be as long as is possible.

The ideal degree of inclination in a good riding shoulder, measuring from the junction of the neck and withers to the point of the shoulder, is estimated at about 60 degrees. From the highest point of the withers to the point of the shoulder 43 degrees, and from point of shoulder to the junction of the withers with the back 40 degrees. To get some idea of the slope of the shoulder hold the end of a piece of string on the point of the shoulder and the other end upon the highest point of the withers, or, if you can manage it, on the posterior angle of the scapula. Measure the distance and observe the angle of inclination and compare some half-dozen horses in this way and you will begin to see the difference.

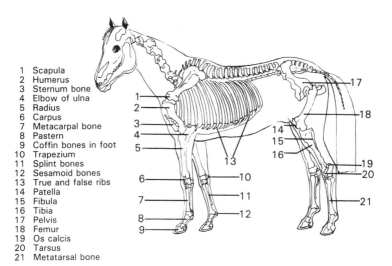

1 Scapula
2 Humerus
3 Sternum bone
4 Elbow of ulna
5 Radius
6 Carpus
7 Metacarpal bone
8 Pastern
9 Coffin bones in foot
10 Trapezium
11 Splint bones
12 Sesamoid bones
13 True and false ribs
14 Patella
15 Fibula
16 Tibia
17 Pelvis
18 Femur
19 Os calcis
20 Tarsus
21 Metatarsal bone

Fig. 4 The horse's skeleton

The scapula, however, is only part of the story. Just as important is the length and position of the connecting humerus. If the latter is short, which is desirable, then the foreleg will be positioned further to the front. If it is long, which is undesirable, then the elbow and the foreleg are placed to the rear and under the forehand. It follows that a long humerus, even when combined with a long, sloped scapula, will result in a shorter stride and a greater degree of knee action, the leg having to be raised and so bent at the knee before it is put down, thus producing more concussion in the limb. *Some* native ponies move in this fashion; most of the Andalusian and their derivatives such as the Lipizzaner; the majority of the coaching breeds and such showy performers as the American exotics, the Saddlebred and Walking Horse, for instance.

A short humerus, combined with a good shoulder, ensures that the foreleg is positioned to the front, thus lengthening the stride and producing a long free action that is not elevated as when the humerus is long, and does not in consequence subject the limb to so great a degree of concussion.

Even with a good shoulder, however, the knee is rarely brought in advance of the point of the shoulder at walk; at trot the knee does not go beyond a line dropped from the poll to the ground. When galloping the forefoot is put down in line with the nose and only very rarely, even when the head and neck are fully extended does the foot fall forward of that point.

A straighter shoulder is permissible and even desirable in draught horses for the reasons already given, but otherwise upright shoulders are to be avoided as inefficient, uncomfortable and potentially damaging to the fore limbs. The endurance of the horse is also diminished by a shoulder of this sort since in order to cover the same distance at the same speed the straight-shouldered horse is compelled to perform more work than his more fortunately endowed brethren.

CHEST

It was once said of the chest by an eminent authority that it could not be too broad. Which, of course, is rubbish. Too wide a chest in a riding horse produces a round, rolling action which is particularly noticeable at the canter and gallop. It is not of such importance in the draught horse, who may very well be wide-chested, since he works only at slow paces. The chest must not, on the other hand, be too narrow giving the appearance of 'both legs coming out of the same hole'. When that is the case it is likely that the forelegs will be so close as to brush against each other causing injury to the joints and lower limbs or, more seriously, for the horse to 'plait', which is when the forelegs are crossed one over the other. In a riding horse that is a most unpleasant and dangerous action.

A simple way of checking out the chest and its relationship with the forelegs is to stand in front of the horse and imagine a line being drawn from the point of the shoulder to the ground. It should pass through the centre of the knee, fetlock and foot. Anything outside of this line denotes a conformational failing which is bound to result in the action being untrue.

TRUNK

The trunk lies behind the withers and shoulder and comprises the back, up to the quarters, which is supported by the dorsal and lumbar vertebrae of the spine. On the latter the weight of the thorax and abdomen depends. When regarding the trunk there are two reliable rules of thumb to provide guidelines. The first one is that the depth of the horse through the girth, ie the measurement from the top of the wither to the deepest part of the body behind the elbow, should be equal to the measurement from that last point to the ground. The second is to measure the back from the rear of the withers to the croup, then measure the distance from the point of the shoulder back to the last of the false ribs (there are eight 'true' ribs at the front of the structure followed by ten 'false' ones). The first should be short and the last one long. The greater the difference the better is the overall proportion. For myself I would like the last measurement to be at least double the first.

Depth of girth allows ample room for the lungs and their expansion. Frequently people talk about 'heart room' in this respect, which really has nothing to do with the matter. There is always plenty of room for the heart but the real concern is with space for the lungs and the respiratory ability.

The girth needs to be as deep as possible in comparison with the length; in fact, its depth should be such as to make the horse look short-legged. A horse that is 'on the leg' and 'shows a lot of daylight' is rarely long in the leg; rather he is lacking in depth of girth.

Obviously, if the horse is to be deep through he must be long in the true ribs. The eight pairs of true ribs (sternal) are attached to both vertebrae and sternum bone, whilst the ten pairs of false ribs (asternal) are attached only to the vertebrae. In the riding horse the true ribs are flatter than the false ones, which should be nicely sprung, so that the rider's thighs and knees lie flat behind the triceps muscles. The false ribs lie over the kidneys and other vital organs and they too need to be fairly long. Short ribs in this area lead up to animals 'running up light' when put into work. In other words the horse looks like a greyhound in the post-abdominal area leading into the quarters. Short ribs and the resulting greyhound shape cause saddles to slip backwards – an inconvenient dilemma in a hill country, for which a breastplate is not an entirely satisfactory solution.

As a final tip for this area, the distance between the last rib and the hip bone should not be more than the breadth of a man's hand. Anything more is termed to be 'short of a rib' and there will be a distinct slackness in the area. Such horses are always difficult to keep in condition and this failing must be regarded as one of the more serious structural weaknesses. Mares, however, are allowed just a shade more length in this part.

Harness horses and those of some of the heavy breeds, particularly perhaps the Clydesdale, have round ribs rather than flat ones like the saddle horse. As a result they are usually lacking in depth through the girth.

The Arab, as usual different again, has an extra pair of ribs, making nineteen, and five instead of the usual six lumbar vertebrae. Because of this you will rarely see an Arab with a slack middle.

BACK

If there was one essential feature in the conformation of the riding horse it would be the ability to carry a saddle. 'If you can't see where you could put a saddle,' said one distinguished judge of horses, 'don't bother to look at anything else.' Of course, he was right. The back must be shaped so that it carries a saddle well and it has to be a structure of sufficient strength to carry the rider's weight.

In perfection we need a back strongly muscled on either side of the spine and rising just slightly to the croup. Strength, however, should not be confused with width and too broad a back, in its relation to the horse's size, is to be avoided. In fact, broad backs may cause saddle fitting problems and they are certainly of little advantage to those of us possessed of short legs.

Faults best avoided are hollow, dropped or 'sway' backs and their opposite, the 'roach' back.

The former are said to give a comfortable ride but they must be regarded as a serious conformational weakness, particularly when they occur in relatively young horses. Backs of this sort are usually associated wth advancing years and are most often seen in old horses.

The roach back, a convex structure, is the stronger of the two extremes, but it can be desperately uncomfortable to ride and it does nothing for the action. Inevitably the stride is shortened and roach-backed horses are usually disposed towards the unfortunate failing of 'forging' or 'clicking', ie the toe of the hind shoe hitting the underside of the toe of the forefoot.

There are then those horses which are described as being 'cold-backed', a euphemism if ever there was one. They will cringe, lowering the back, when a saddle is put on and they may even sit down when being mounted. Of course, it has nothing to do with the back being 'cold'. The reason for such behaviour is because the back has suffered some damage or because of an arthritic condition (which is by no means uncommon) in the transverse processes of the last three vertebrae and in their junction with the sacrum. The problem can be overcome partially by using a thick numnah, saddling up some ten minutes previous to the horse being required and then walking him round for a further few minutes before the rider, taking care not to put his full weight in the saddle immediately, mounts the horse.

There is no way of detecting the cold-backed horse by visual appraisal, but a hand passed firmly over the back will cause the horse to wince noticeably and is revealing of some difficulty in this important area.

The length of the back used to be a subject which caused differences of opinion amongst horsemen, many of whom at one time were in favour of a shorter back rather than a longer one.

Today, it is generally agreed that a little length in the back (more length, of course, is permissible in a mare than a gelding or stallion) is no bad thing and such a back will be less susceptible to damage than one of the opposite sort. Frequently, some length in this department is accompanied by powerful loins and quarters and so long as these are present and there is no inclination towards slackness behind the saddle the structure is acceptable enough.

A longer back will, of course, contribute to speed because it will allow the hindlegs to be brought further under the body to produce a correspondingly greater length of stride.

The short back, in theory, must be the stronger structure, but it can have serious disadvantages. In its extremes it can be most uncomfortable for the rider who will receive much of the propulsive thrust of the quarters in his seat. It is certainly not conducive to speed because of the limitation it imposes on the stride of the hindlegs. A short back is less able to absorb concussion and therefore more prone to being damaged, and it may also result in an undesirable shortening of the thorax.

Very recently there has been much discussion about the flexibility of the horse's spine. The conclusion that there is no flexibility, or virtually none, being looked upon as some major revelation, particularly by the dressage exponents who for years have been encouraging us to 'bend the horse round the inside leg'. In fairness, most of us have embraced that impossible ideal, using it to encourage a mental attitude in riders when they are changing the direction of the movement or riding circles. The fact that the horse's spine is a rigid construction, making it impossible to 'bend the horse uniformly throughout his length from poll to tail', has been acknowledged ever since the first studies were made into the skeleton structure of the equine. The only flexion possible, and it is so minimal as to be almost irrelevant, is between the last of the dorsal and the first of the lumbar joints and between the first, second and third lumbar vertebrae. A little movement is possible between the last lumbar bone and the sacrum.

It is possible, nonetheless, for the horse to give the *impression* of being bent round the inside leg for the reason that when a turn is being made the muscles on the inside of the body will be flattened, whilst those on the outside of the body will swell, as it were, in corresponding fashion.

If a certain length in the back is both permissible and desirable, it is not so when it comes to considering the *loin,* which is the area between the saddle and the croup. It has to be very strong, the muscles forming it being thick, short and powerful, because upon it depends much of the propulsive force of the quarters. It has to be broad, never narrow, since it covers the vital organs. If it is overly long there will be a space between the last rib and the angle of the haunch, or if you would rather, the pin bone, with a prominent hollow in front of the latter. The horse is then 'slack' instead of being 'well-ribbed-up'.

The *croup* is the highest part of the quarter and in the mature horse is usually in line with the wither, although as we have seen previously it is possible for there to be variations to the norm.

Where the croup is high, in the formation called a 'goose-rump', a sloping effect will be given to the quarters which may give the appearance of the tail being set low, which is considered to be not only unsightly but a sign of weakness in the quarters. In fact, this is not the case with a goose-rump. It may be less than aesthetically pleasing but it indicates good bone development, advantageous for the attachment of muscle, and it usually goes with a horse possessed of jumping ability. In Arab horses, and possibly in their near-derivatives as well, the croup is long and level with the sacrum tipped slightly upwards to ensure the significantly high tail placement which is a prized characteristic of the breed. In the Thoroughbred horse the sacrum tilts a little downwards and the tail is therefore placed in a lower position. The Continental horses, in particular the German breeds, tend towards the more level croup and high tail carriage which characterises the Arab, and one can appreciate why it is that despite great strength in the quarters they are not exactly speed merchants since those posterior limbs are placed behind the position in which they can best be employed for moving at speed – but then not all of us want or need to operate in top gear all the time.

A very low-set tail and a pronounced slope from the croup so that a mean appearance is given to the quarter is best avoided since it is indicative of general weakness in the area.

QUARTERS

All this, of course, leads us to the examination of the quarters as a whole, and they are best viewed from a point directly behind the horse. The impression should be one of roundness at the top, a pear shape widening into muscular, very strongly developed second thighs (gaskins). One can look at the quarters from this viewpoint in terms of two squares, as shown in Fig. 5 below. The sides of each square should, in perfection, equal the length of the head. If a vertical line is drawn from the fetlocks upwards through the centre of the hocks the limbs should in no way deviate from that line.

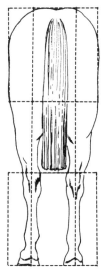

The sides of each square equal the length of the horse's head. The upright line passes through the centre of the hocks and fetlocks

Fig. 5 The hindquarters

Hips should not protrude noticeably and they must be level. A horse that drops a hip is said to have a 'dropped pin'. Usually that means some damage has been sustained, possibly as a result of the horse banging a hip against a door post, and almost invariably there will be unlevelness in the gaits.

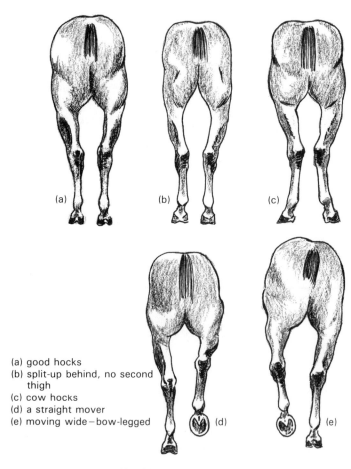

(a) good hocks
(b) split-up behind, no second thigh
(c) cow hocks
(d) a straight mover
(e) moving wide – bow-legged

Fig. 6 Hock placements

If when viewed from the rear the juncture of the thighs is high up under the tail with a lot of 'daylight' between them the condition is termed 'split up behind'. It is caused by a thin under-developed gaskin, indicative of weakness rather than strength in this essential part of the riding horse's anatomy. It is the muscles of the quarters which operate the hindlegs, and these muscles in conjunction with those of the second thigh provide the necessary power for jumping. If a horse that is poor in these respects is required to jump he will naturally enough not be a very efficient or athletic performer. Furthermore, he is almost certain to develop irregularities and even diseases in the joints of the hindlegs as a result.

HOCKS

The appearance of strength in the quarters is important in assessing the potential of the horse, but the placement of the leg in relation to the hip and the positioning and shape of the hock is critical to the performance. The hock, after all, is probably the hardest-worked joint in

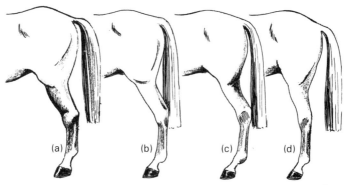

(a) good hindleg, good length from hip to point of buttock, good second thigh
(b) sickle hock, no second thigh
(c) hocks too high, no length from hip to point of buttock and hip to point of hock
(d) hocks too straight

Fig. 7 The hindlegs

the horse's body and it needs to be paid considerable attention on that account.

Maximum efficiency with the minimum risk of strain will be achieved, so long as all else is equal, when the point of the hock is in line with the chestnut that lies just above the knee of the foreleg. The second thigh must then be long and the hock set low because of the shortness of the hind cannon. In the ideal hindleg a line from the point of the buttock to the ground should touch the point of the hock and then coincide with the vertical line formed by the rear of the cannon bone. Such an arrangement should make for maximum leverage in the components of the leg and therefore greater speed.

In practice it may not always be so. Some very fast Thoroughbred horses have their hocks higher off the ground than makes for perfection and may also be higher at the croup than the wither. No one, however, would pretend that was a conformation suitable for a comfortable riding horse. Quite a lot of good jumpers and hunters have their hocks slightly in advance of the line of perfection and the cannon bone similarly placed forward of the vertical. The ability to gallop fast is then reduced but the increase in the possible articulation of the joints and the greater strength afforded, provides additional thrust for jumping and it would also be a suitable placement for a dressage horse.

Faults in the hock are when they are obviously overbent and curved on the front surface (sickle hocks) and when they are carried well to the rear of the vertical line dropped from the point of the buttock. This last condition is referred to, very graphically, as 'hocks being in the next county'. Both faults predispose the joint to uneven wear and extra strain which can result in disease and damage. Additionally, there is a noticeable lack of propulsive power combined with an inability for

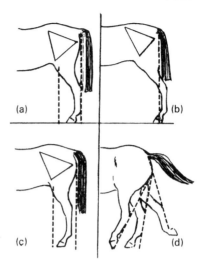

(a) normal hock placement
(b) hocks 'in the next county'
(c) over-straight hock and stifle
(d) in movement the rear of the cannon corresponds to the line from the seat bone

Fig. 8 The hocks

the hocks to be fully engaged under the body. It is also possible for hocks to be too straight. In these instances a line dropped from the seat bone would pass a little behind the edge of the flexor tendon and behind the cannon bone. This condition, too, results in uneven wear, some loss of propulsive power and subjects the limb to greater concussion.

There are then 'bowed' hocks, where the points are carried far apart and the lower limbs carried inside a line dropped from the point to the ground, and 'cow-hocks', where the points almost touch each other. Both reduce the speed potential, since the limbs cannot move straight to their front, and both conditions cause uneven wear in the mechanism of the joint. Nonetheless it is possible that whilst the joint stands up to the strains imposed upon it the performance, other than in respect of speed, is not too greatly affected. The Clydesdale, for instance, is often cow-hocked but still has a considerable reputation as a worker in heavy draught. For all that, hocks, or any other joints which are out-of-true are best avoided if possible.

Joints, we are told frequently, should be large. That is very true and in no regard more so than in the hock which has to absorb the very considerable concussion to which the hind limb is subjected and which has so much weight to carry. The larger the joint, within reason, the greater will be the surface area available to absorb the concussive effect. Like feet and knees, hocks need to be an exact pair. This may seem to be an elementary point to make but it is one of the most important to observe in making an assessment of a horse or pony. Where one joint is smaller than the other it is more probable that it is caused by injury or disease than by any congenital defect.

It is possible, for all that, for a joint, particularly the hocks, to be *too* large. They then appear lumpy, fleshy and generally soft and lymphatic, rather like a pair of overworked human legs with circulatory problems. Hocks of this sort occur most frequently where there is a high percentage of cart blood, as in some heavyweight horses. The effect of such hocks is to put the whole leg out of balance, limiting the joint's flexion and restricting the action.

FORELEGS

There is a tendency in teaching circles to place, I think, too much emphasis on the hindleg and its engagement. This latter is a vital requirement, but the importance of the foreleg should not be underestimated and certainly not ignored. Both sets of limbs are necessary in locomotion and the front ones play just as big a part in jumping as the hind ones. Indeed, in the first stage of the jump it is the muscles of the forearm, working with those of the loin, which are responsible initially for lifting the body, and its human burden, and propelling it forward.

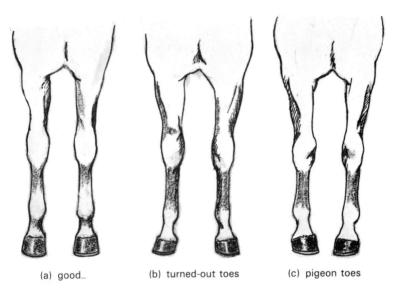

(a) good (b) turned-out toes (c) pigeon toes

Fig. 9 Foreleg placements

Before looking at the forelegs in detail it is best to take a look at them from the front to satisfy oneself as to their placement in relation to the body and their overall straightness. Anything out-of-true here must clearly place undue strain on the limb, wherein, after all, lie the principal sources of lameness.

Starting at the top of the leg the first concern is with the elbow, the position of which depends upon the length of the humerus bone. If the movement of the foreleg is to be free and unhampered it is essential for the elbow to stand well clear of the ribs. It will then be possible for the leg to be carried well forward, as the whole of the shoulder is moved. If, conversely, it should lie hard up against the ribs, so that one cannot comfortably get a fist between the limb and the body at the point of juncture, the elbow is termed as being 'tied-in'. That means that the shoulder movement will be restricted and action made possible only from the elbow. Should the elbow be set back a long way the spine (and the rider) will be subjected to greater concussion. Any failing in the position of the elbow throws extra strain on the hocks which have to do more work to compensate for the faulty action of the forelimbs.

The forearm has to be strong, very well muscled and of such a length as to allow the knee to be carried as low as possible on short cannon bones.

Knees, like hocks, need to be large and, in addition, as flat as possible on their surface, whilst, of course, remaining in proportion to the rest of the leg. Such knees, which have well-defined pisiform bones, provide a carpal sheath (a channel, in effect) which will be broad enough to carry the flexor tendon without it becoming pinched. Small round knees almost invariably accompany chronic tendon problems.

To ensure straight movement knees have to be perpendicular throughout their length and they have to be absolutely straight in relation to the rest of the leg.

Like hocks again, the knees must be a pair. One that is smaller than the other is an indication of incipient trouble, since the smaller one will have been exposed to a greater degree of strain. Possibly, the worst fault in the lower limb is that which is described as a 'calf knee', also sometimes referred to as 'back of the knee'. It is applied to a leg which curves inwards below the knee. It is a sure source, not surprisingly, of tendon problems and it does nothing to help absorb concussion. It is, indeed, an abomination.

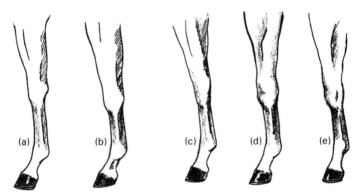

(a) light of bone, long cannons, small knee, tied-in below the knee
(b) good foreleg with good flat bone, large knee, fluted tendons, average pastern, well-developed forearm
(c) small knee, back of the knee weak
(d) good foreleg with well-developed trapezium bone
(e) over at the knee

Fig. 10 The forelegs

Almost as bad is the horse which is 'tied-in below the knee'. This is when the measurement below the knee is less than that taken lower down nearer the fetlock joint, and it constricts the proper passage of tendons, to their obvious detriment.

There are also horses which are 'over at the knee' like those in the nineteenth-century prints of worn-out cab horses. The cannon slopes back below the knee so that the knee itself seems to be inclined forward. Quite often the condition is caused by hard work but sometimes it is part and parcel of the individual's make and shape. However it comes about, it seems to have no ill effect and it is held that horses exhibiting this peculiarity rarely suffer a tendon breakdown.

Knees which are high off the ground are thus positioned because of the length of the cannon bone — a serious failing because length below the knee must point to an inherent structural weakness. The strongest

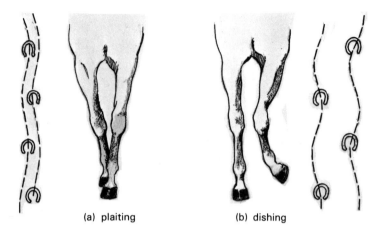

(a) plaiting   (b) dishing

Fig. 11 Foreleg action

construction is a short thick one and this is what is required in the *cannon,* so long, of course, as it remains in proportion. It does, however, need to be the same circumference from top to bottom which brings us to that well-loved but not always so well understood horsy topic, *bone.* It is bone, combined with the horse's general build, which is the principal factor in judging the horse's capacity to carry weight. The height has little or nothing to do with it.

Obviously, there is no sure method of calculating the weight-carrying capacity and when breed societies and others stipulate 'flat, dense bone', or even 'good, flinty bone' it is just so much pie-in-the-sky. There is no way of knowing, short of cutting off a leg, whether the bone is dense or otherwise and I very much doubt whether we really know what we refer to when we use the words flat or flinty. Density and strength of bone are more easily understood. Bone is like a tube, the central core of which is filled with marrow. Its strength varies in accordance with the thickness and density of the surrounding structure, the strongest bone being that with the smallest central core and the thickest and least porous surrounding wall.

We measure 'bone' below the knee but, of course, the measurement round the leg includes a composite structure of ligaments, tendons and tissues which surround the bone. There is no way of actually measuring the circumference of the bone itself.

In times past there was a simple formula which stated as follows: 8ins (20cm) below the knee carries up to 11-12st (70-80kg); 9-10ins (23-25cm) carries 13-14st (80-90kg); and 10-11ins (25-28cm) carries 15st (95kg) and over.

Of course, that couldn't take account of the bone's density or of its thickness about the central core. It is held that the bone of Arabs, for instance, as well as Thoroughbreds, Welsh Mountain ponies and the like is denser than that of more common-bred animals and the central core much smaller.

Obviously, we need 'bone', if by that we mean a good measurement round a short cannon, if the limbs are going to carry the horse's body weight as well as that of a rider, but we should not perhaps be too dogmatic or too presumptuous, having regard for the quality of bone and the existence of its covering structures.

What is certain is that the cannons should feel cool to the touch and hard. There should be no puffiness which might give the impression of the cannon being *round* instead of *flat*.

The same, of course, applies to the *fetlock* joint, which like all the joints should be large and well-formed. The fetlocks should be flat on their sides and once more there should be no sign of their being filled. These joints do, in fact, tell us a great deal about the amount of work the horse has done and how his limbs have stood up to the demands made of them.

The fetlock runs into the *pastern,* a remarkably efficient shock-absorber. Short, upright pasterns, often found in common-bred horses and ponies are not to be recommended since they will be unable to do their job and save the limb from being jarred. Very upright pasterns can, indeed, lead to a variety of unsoundnesses caused by concussion.

At the opposite end of the scale there is the over-long pastern, sometimes seen in both Arab and Thorough-bred horses. They make for a very comfortable ride but as with any exaggerated feature in the horse's confor-mation they have to be viewed as a potential weakness. The ideal is something between the two extremes with the hind pasterns being a little shorter than the front ones because of the compensating flexion of the hock. Where this latter is unduly straight the pastern frequently compensates for the deficiency by being long. It is thus able, to a degree, to save the hock joint from the effects of jarring.

FEET

Napoleon said that armies marched on their stomachs. Horses have regard for their inner needs also, but they walk, trot, canter, gallop and jump on their feet and of all the horsey maxims none is more true than that which says 'no foot, no 'oss'.

There are departures from the ideal conformation which can be acceptable but no one could ever be advised to buy a horse with suspect feet. Since possibly 75 per cent of cases of lameness in shod horses are concerned with the foot, intending purchasers would do well to examine this part of the horse with extra care.

First and foremost the feet in front and behind should be exact pairs. Where one foot is smaller than the other or differently shaped it is more than likely that there has been some lameness at some time. A foot can become smaller than its partner due to injury or disease. If the foot is painful the horse will naturally attempt to ease the discomfort by putting his weight on his sound leg. The damaged foot not being subjected to the spreading pressures on the sound one will then shrink and the frog will shrivel if the condition persists over a long period or is chronic.

Small 'boxy' feet which look to be too small for their owner are best avoided as being more prone to disease. The horn of the foot has to be strong and thick so that there is plenty of room for the shoe nails to be hammered in without fear of the foot being damaged. Brittle feet, badly broken ones and those showing longitudinal cracks should be treated with suspicion. A noticeable ringed appearance of the hoof is even more serious since it is a sure sign that the horse has suffered an attack of laminitis, that most painful and crippling of inflammatory hoof conditions.

White feet, which accompany white legs, are thought to be of softer horn than those where the wall is either grey or even slate blue and so are considered more prone to wear. Whether that is so is probably debatable and I would not myself turn away a horse because of white feet.

An inspection of the underside of the foot should show deep and open heels. There should be no suggestion of the foot being contracted in this area. The bars are particularly important since if they are not well defined the heel itself will be shallow.

The sole in the forefeet is slightly concave and in the hindfeet more so. In both cases it has to be thick so that damage will not be caused by rough going. Flat or dropped soles are obviously more easily bruised and damaged and horses with this failing can be a source of constant trouble.

The frog, which is the foot's anti-concussion device

and also prevents slipping, has to be large and well-formed if it is to do its job satisfactorily. If the frog is small and shrivelled it will not, of course, make contact with the ground and it will be impossible for it to perform its proper function.

In the riding horse the angle of slope on the foot is generally agreed as being 50 degrees for the forefeet and between 55 and 60 degrees in the hind ones.

The weight-carrying parts of the foot are the walls, the bars and outer edges of the sole and the frog; all need to be well-formed and healthy if the foot is to function satisfactorily.

All four feet should face directly to the front, the toes being neither turned in or out, if the action is to be true and mechanically efficient. Feet which turn out are the more serious fault of the two because in movement they are likely to brush against each other. There is a theory that horses with turned-in toes go better in deep and holding conditions but I have never found a satisfactory explanation of why this should be so.

Action

Conformation is about movement and it is always necessary to see a horse trotted and walked out away from you and towards you. Additionally you need to view him from the side. In movement it is easier to see whether the limbs are carried in a straight line with the body and whether the feet turn one way or another.

If the horse is flexing each joint properly it should be possible to see the sole of each foot at some time during every stride.

The stifle gives a pretty sure indication of faulty hock action. If it remains in line with the body all is well but if it is 'punched' outwards as the joint flexes the hocks are usually being turned inwards.

The levelness of the hock action can be checked by viewing the horse from the side. The point of each hock should rise to the same height when the joint is flexed. If one is lower than the other then you may suspect the presence of a spavin.

The shoes will also tell you a lot about the action. Obviously, the wear on the shoes will be even if the action is true. Watch particularly for a hind shoe with the toe showing more signs of wear than its partner. When this occurs it is an indication of an imperfect flexion of the joint.

For hunting and jumping one can forgive some un-straightness in the action all else being equal and if the price is right. For the show ring or for dressage one would be far less tolerant. In both pursuits, particularly the latter, straight level movement and maximum joint flexion must be an important consideration. It would be a waste of time and money to attempt the advanced schooling of a dressage horse if the joints, particularly those of the hocks, were incapable of flexion to the full degree.

7   Blemishes and Defects

Spavins, splints, corns, mallenders, sallenders etc, etc,
being all curable are beneath your notice. A few of these
little infirmities in your stable is always a subject of
conversation – and you may, perhaps, now and then
want one.

'Geoffrey Gambado'
(Sir Wm. Bunbury) 1750-1811
An Academy for Grown Horsemen

Reference has already been made to conformational
failings which predispose the horse to disease or chronic
ailments. Of course, a veterinary examination before
purchase will reveal those defects which can be seen or
felt, but it is prudent to know something about the more
common ones, where they occur and how they can be
recognised.

For the most part the conditions with which an
intending purchaser is concerned will be connected with
the limbs and lameness which arises as a result of
damage or disease in them. In these days, when horses
are asked to jump nearly to their ultimate capacity over
fences often sited on ground that is far from level, there
is an increasing incidence of back injury, but that is a
complication best left to the veterinary surgeon. So long
as the horse rides without sign of discomfort and feels to
be using his back there is no reason for the buyer to feel
concern. After all, if there is a severe back injury, it will
probably be obvious enough to prohibit the horse being

offered for sale. It could, of course, be disguised by the use of drugs, but a routine blood test during veterinary examination would soon reveal their presence.

One of the most common blemishes in the horse is a *splint*. In the simplest terms this is a bony enlargement on the cannon bone, or splint bones, of either the fore or hindlegs. Usually they occur on the former and rarely appear after the age of five. They are caused by work which involves jarring or concussion, and only cause lameness in their formative stage, when there will be heat in the area. Once the splint is 'set' it causes no further trouble and is no more than a little unsightly. The only time that a splint might cause a problem is when it occurs high up under the knee and could therefore interfere with the movement of that joint.

Sidebone is the name given to an ossification at the side of the foot. It is said to be confined to the heavier type of horse and is caused once more by our old friend concussion. Obviously, therefore, a heavily built animal moving with pronounced knee action would be more prone to the condition. However, although lameness may occur initially it is only temporary and once the preliminary stages are passed the horse will most usually be sound again.

Ringbone is an arthritic condition of the fetlock. Where it affects the pastern joint it is called high ringbone; if it occurs between the pedal bone and the pastern it is low ringbone. In both instances the new bone formed round the joint can be easily felt with the fingers. The horse will be lame on rough ground, if turned in a tight circle or moved from side to side. The lameness is usually progressive and it would be unwise to buy a horse suspected of having ringbone without veterinary advice.

When the sesamoid bones in the fetlock joint suffer concussion and become inflamed as a result a condition called *sesamoiditis* occurs. A hard swelling is apparent on the joint and initially the horse is in pain. A cure can be effected but the horse is usually left with a 'pottery' action in front and lameness may recur as work increases.

Pedal ostitis concerns an acute inflammation of the pedal bone within the foot. Initially lameness is caused and the sole of the foot will be very sensitive. It does not necessarily, however, cause permanent lameness and is relatively easy to treat with modern drugs.

Navicular disease is rather more permanent and unpleasant but can be treated to a degree by the use of an anticoagulant. Inevitably, however, the condition deteriorates to the point where nothing further can be done.

It is known that the cause of navicular is decay in the bone as a result of it receiving an insufficient supply of blood, but why it occurs is less certain. Signs of the onset of the disease are intermittent lameness followed by a pointing of the affected limb, ie the horse eases pressure on the damaged limb by placing it in advance of the other and leaning his body backward, and it seems that the disease is usually accompanied by contracted boxy feet. It occurs more usually in the forefeet and in horses over the age of eight years.

Laminitis, which was mentioned previously (p. 125), is easily recognised by the ringed, concave condition of the foot wall.

Corns in the horse, causing lameness, are more prevalent than one would think and without doubt some horses are more predisposed to them than others. Often, a corn, which is a bruising on the angle of the sole at the heel of the foot ('seat of corn') is caused by faulty shoeing which puts pressure on the sole rather than on the wall of the foot. Remedial shoes can be fitted to take pressure off the seat of the corn but a horse with a history of corn trouble should be thought about carefully. Persistent corns are an expensive nuisance and one would want some pretty substantial compensating factors to put up with them.

Sore shins, resulting in a swelling on the front of the cannon, are usually confined to young horses in work but the condition though initially painful disappears with rest. If the complaint becomes extended into *epiphysitis,* an inflammation of the growth plate in the bone, some swelling may be left. Young horses who are fed (incorrectly) to produce a big top (body) at an early age are more prone to this condition than those allowed to 'grow on' and develop naturally.

Tendon troubles are accompanied by swelling and heat in cases of strain. A complete breakdown occurs when the superficial and deep tendons are ruptured; obviously, a potential buyer would cease to be that if the horse had 'broken down', but it is possible that a buyer may be presented with a horse which has a 'bowed tendon'. This is not necessarily a sign of immediate trouble but warning bells should ring very loudly since further work may result in more serious damage leading to a full rupturing.

Swollen or filled legs which occur in old horses are not the result of tendon problems but are due to general wear and tear and a consequent congestion of blood in the lower limbs.

In the hindleg there are a number of defects concerned with that much over-worked joint, the hock. Principal among these are spavins and curbs and the bursal enlargements such as thoropin and capped hocks.

A *bone spavin* is a bony enlargement on the inside of the hock caused by severe inflammation and osteo-arthritis between the adjacent bones. It is the result of work on a joint which is not, perhaps because of its placement, ideally suited to that purpose. The flexion of the joint is affected, the toe being dragged, and the horse becomes more or less permanently lame as the disease progresses.

The test for spavin is a simple one. The foot is picked up and the hock joint held in a flexed position for half a minute or so. When the leg is released and the horse trotted away lameness will be quite apparent. Treatment can alleviate the condition considerably but a spavined horse is not the one to buy.

The other spavin is called a *bog spavin,* a simple bursal enlargement which appears as a soft swelling on the front of the hock. It is neither painful nor causes lameness, but it is a sign of wear often associated with upright hocks.

A *curb* is a swelling or a thickening on the back of the hock just under its point. It is due to a sprain of the plantar ligament which joins the cannon to the hock bones immediately above it. Horses with sickle-hocks are more susceptible to this injury than others, but it can occur if the hock is over-extended when jumping or when some other sort of sudden stress is imposed on the hind leg.

Initially the horse will be lame but after rest will go sound again. The thickening, however, remains and plantar ligaments which have once suffered a sprain may do so again in circumstances which place the joint under stress.

Bursal enlargements are exemplified in *thoropin,* at the back of the hock, *windgalls* round the fetlock joints, *capped hocks* on the point of the hock, and the *bog spavin* which has been mentioned.

A bursa is a sack of fluid which acts as a buffer for ligament, tendon or muscle passing over bone. When the sack is stretched through pressure it fills with fluid and causes a swelling which does not cause lameness but which is a sign of wear and tear (except in the case of a capped hock or a capped elbow which may be caused by a blow in the stable or when travelling).

To detect lameness is not difficult if the condition is acute; it is far more difficult if it is a matter of a horse going 'unlevel'.

Nonetheless, it is in most cases possible to detect if one follows the set routine of having the horse trotted towards and away.

When lameness is suspected in front have the horse trotted towards you without the handler holding the head to one side or holding the rein close to the bit or headcollar. On a loose rein the poll of a lame horse will rise and fall, the lame leg coming to the ground as the poll rises. To detect lameness in the hindlegs have the horse trotted away and keep your eye on the highest part of the rump. If it rises and falls lameness is present, the lame leg being the one which hits the ground as the rump rises.

Of course, a veterinary examination will reveal a lameness but there is no point in having a vet if you can see for yourself that the horse is lame, not, that is, unless you want the horse badly and suspect the injury to be no more than minor.

It is not, I think, sensible to accept the explanation for lameness offered to a friend of mine by a young lady whose horse he went to see following an eulogistic advert in the equestrian press. When my friend suggested that the horse was lame, the young lady replied: 'Oh, that's nothing to worry about, he always trots like that.' Quite so, but she didn't sell him.

The other unsoundnesses to be avoided are those concerned with the respiratory diseases. Indeed, in these days of myriad 'flu viruses one would urge purchasers never to buy a horse with a cough. If you want the horse wait till the vendor will guarantee it free from any sort of respiratory disorder.

Broken wind, which nowadays is called Chronic Obstructive Pulmonary Disease (COPD) rather than emphysema (which is really a permanent breakdown of the lung tissue), reduces the ability of the horse to work at other than very slow speeds, in fact, a walk. It can be treated now, but a broken-winded horse is not worth buying.

Horses that roar or whistle do so because of an affection of the main nerves of the larynx. It can in some cases be cured by the Hobday operation and one imagines that no one would Hobday a horse that was not a good one in other respects. Horses can, however, 'make a noise' without it detracting from the performance and without therefore an operation being necessary. However, *don't* take the vendor's word for it, insist instead on a certificate from a vet which states that no operation is considered necessary. Finally, do make sure that the horse you buy is not a sufferer from *sweet-itch,* which is a highly irritating allergic dermatitis stimulated by biting insects during the spring and summer, the insects being most active during the early hours of the morning and in the late evening. A bald neck and/or dock, often raw, are the tell-tale signs of sweet-itch and it takes a long time for the hair to grow again. There are substances and drugs to alleviate the condition but the real answer is to keep the horse stabled, at least whilst the insects are active, and even then some form of repellant treatment will be needed. If you are prepared to go to that trouble, and a good deal more, do, of course, buy the horse – I would think twice.

(The mallenders and sallenders referred to in the heading to this chapter are names given to skin inflammation occurring at the back of the knee and in front of the hock respectively. Modern medication ensures that they can be cleared up very effectively.)

8 The Horse's Vision

His eye, which scornfully glisters like a fire,
Shows his hot courage and his high desire.
                    William Shakespeare (1564-1616)
                                    Venus and Adonis

It is not necessary to know a great deal about equine vision in order to buy a horse satisfactorily, except to bear in mind that the position of the eyes in the head is a critical factor in the type of vision the horse has. Nonetheless, if one has never appreciated what and how the horse sees it can come as something of a shock to understand how well the horse cooperates with us despite having a visionary capability far different to our own. It is for that reason that this chapter has been included.

In most animals the eyes are able to focus because of the ciliary muscle which alters the shape of the eye's lens. In the horse this muscle is far less developed and so a different method of focussing has to be employed.

To a large degree effective focussing in the horse depends upon how the eyes are positioned in the head and upon the width of the forehead separating them. (When I say effective focussing I mean the sort of focus which best suits our needs as regards general performance levels.)

How much the horse sees *below* the level of the head is dependent upon the way in which the latter is joined to the neck and on the length and width of his face.

Because of the shape of the face it is reasonable to assume that a horse will rarely see the contents of a manger set at chest height, nor, of course, will he be able to see his own feet (a failing he shares with some members of the human race, if for different reasons).

It is interesting how for the sake of appearance many horses are deprived of the use of the whiskers growing round the muzzle. Deprived is the right word here, for these whiskers have a purpose. They perform a function rather like a radar beam, assisting the horse to gauge the distance of objects, and food, from his mouth. In other words they compensate for the limited vision afforded by his eyes – so we, who know better, cut them off!

In the heavy horse, whose eyes are set on the side of a wide face, lateral vision is correspondingly increased at the expense of frontal vision. In varying degrees, dependent upon the shape of the face, this will apply, also, to the heavier type of riding horse who has inherited some part of the heavy-horse characteristic in this respect.

The lighter type of riding horse, with possibly more Thoroughbred blood in his background, is much narrower in the forehead than the draught horse and the eyes are placed more to the front. In consequence, although he still has the ability to see to either side using the eyes independently, he has much better frontal vision, which is an advantage in a riding horse who may be expected to jump.

In the horse eyes and ears operate in conjunction. When the horse pricks his ears and points them forward, his eyes also look forward and are centred on the object which has attracted his attention. *The closer the ears are placed together the better will be the forward vision.*

Unlike humans horses are able to use their eyes independently, each being capable of a high degree of lateral vision. This is part of the horse's defensive

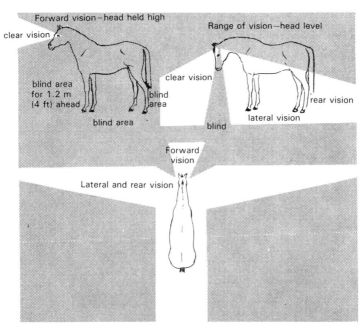

Fig. 12 Limits of forward and lateral vision.
NB it is not possible to have both simultaneously

equipment and a further extension is the ability, because of the eye placement, to see behind him when his head is lowered in the act of grazing. However, when he wishes to focus on objects to his front the head has to be raised. The further away the object, the higher the head has to be raised in order for the eyes to focus effectively.

An appreciation of that point should give riders a better understanding of the need to allow freedom of the head if the horse is to have a clear sight of what is in front: restrictive martingales, or hands, will not be conducive to a proper view of a fence.

In fact, if the horse is allowed reasonable freedom of the head, he sees a fence clearly with both eyes at a distance of 45 ft (13.5 m). Four feet away from the fence (a little over 1 m) his own head, because of its shape and size, prevents him from seeing the obstacle with both eyes simultaneously. As a result he has to tilt his head to one side or another so as to get a sight of it with one eye.

Vision is, in fact, improved if the horse carries his head in a somewhat overbent position, which is often the case with a trained showjumper, but otherwise one must sometimes be forced to conclude that many of our horses jump blind in varying degrees.

Diseases of the Eye

Although horses are relatively free from ocular problems, the eyelids being equipped with very powerful muscles which close the eye very rapidly in case of need and the eye being further protected by a nictating membrane, a third eyelid which can be moved across the eyeball without the lid being closed, the eye is sensitive to injury through bruising and the presence of foreign bodies.

If the cornea is inflamed (the transparent covering of the eye) the affected area shows an opaque film. More severe injuries will result in the eye becoming bloodshot as a result of red blood vessels spreading across its surface.

It is not really possible for the layman to detect eye injuries or diseases beyond those described; an examination of the eyes will, however, be included in the overall examination made by the veterinary surgeon.

9 Colour – Height – Sex

A good horse is never a bad colour.

Anon

Colour

Colour has to be a matter of personal preference but one imagines that few horses (though certainly not all) would be turned down because of their coat colour, if they were otherwise good performers.

There are, of course, prejudices against particular colours: palominos, skewbalds, piebalds and spotted horses (the Appaloosa) are not the most popular in the firm-upper-lip society of hunting England, though they go down very well in the more colourful, outgoing horse world of America. Chesnut mares, like red-haired ladies, are supposed to be fiery and explosive, but that is certainly not true of them all.

There is, indeed, an enormous amount of advice on colour contained in equestrian literature, most of which is contradictory, although nearly all seem to be agreed on the inadvisability of having a horse with four white legs. The three pieces of advice, if they can be termed so, which remain in my own memory are those given by an admittedly prejudiced grandfather: 'Grey horses', he used to say, 'are for rich men' (he was thinking about cleaning them).

'If you must make a fool of yourself, do it on a bay horse, it's less noticeable', which is, I suppose, one explanation for the prejudice against the more exotically coloured, and therefore noticeable, animal.

Finally, 'I won't have a black horse – time enough for one of those b——— when they draw me to my grave'.

More practical is the advice that whatever the colour let it be a good strong one. Wishy-washy colours, particularly the pale shades of chesnut, are usually associated with weak constitutions, although there is no proof of the assertion beyond the experience of generations of horsemen.

Dun, the colouring of the primitive horse, is thought to be found in hardy, enduring horses and there is some reason for the prejudice against coloured horses other than that given.

Many of the skewbalds and piebalds are very common in appearance and the colour does not appear in well-bred horses. On the other hand a good, well-made coloured horse is usually a very good one indeed. A picture of just such a one appears on page 60.

The principal colours in horses are black, bay, brown and chesnut, doubtful cases being decided by the colour of the hair on the muzzle. There are, of course, many others – duns, roans, greys, spots, Palomino and so on – and the source of all colour lies in the individual genes, of which there are thirty-nine, and they are capable of several thousand possible combinations.

Size and Height

The relevance of height and size is to the corresponding proportions of the rider – or that is what it should be. A big heavyweight man needs a horse of the same proportions, whilst a lightweight young lady will do just as well, and probably better, on a horse more suited to her height and weight.

It is a mistake to imagine that 'a good big 'un will always beat a good little 'un' and must therefore be the more desirable acquisition. In fact, big horses have a number of disadvantages. In the first place they are more expensive to feed; in the second they take longer to mature and are therefore more at risk in terms of damage to their component parts if they are worked too young. On the whole they lack the natural balance of their smaller, handier and usually more athletic counterparts.

It does not follow that the extra power obtained from a larger frame and bigger muscles is necessarily equal to the additional weight which has to be carried. It may be, indeed, that the weight factor is in excess of the physical effort which can be applied.

The failing, I believe, in some of the big Continental Warm-Bloods is their lack of stamina. Many of them are splendid 'three-hour horses' but are not as good in terms of sustained effort as the sharp Thoroughbred sort.

Furthermore the very big horse is often more disposed to that sort of heavy throat formation which leads to respiratory problems.

The smaller horse, with less body weight to bother about, is usually the better balanced and those with a dash of pony blood are immeasurably more clever over fences and across country. In addition they are more responsive, receptive and intelligent than the really big horse who may suffer in these respects from his cold-blood ancestry.

The only real advantage of the big horse is that he may add to the ego of his rider and may, perhaps, make the fences look smaller.

Sex

The sex of a horse contributes to some slight variations in form, outside of the normal genital differences. In general, the female is longer in the back than the male and has to be wider in the pelvic area. A long level croup in a mare is not desirable because this formation will make parturition more difficult. A mare should have a feminine look about her, in contrast to the more aggressive presence of the male. She does not have the characteristic crest of the stallion, for instance. A gelding does not have this crested neck either unless castration has been delayed, a procedure which is sometimes advocated in the case of a horse intended for showing or dressage. Mares, however, are, by reason of the natural sexual cycle, less temperamentally predictable than males.

The mare comes into season in the Western Hemisphere every three weeks between February and October. During these periods she can become touchy and irritable. Highly sexed mares are particularly troublesome in this respect and even ones less affected by the cycle will lose concentration in their work. For this reason mares are not considered to be very suitable for dressage and other competitive disciplines. There will, however, always be the exception. Nonetheless it is worth while making enquiries about a mare's behaviour during the time she is in-season.

On the other hand, because of her breeding potential, a mare must be the better long-term proposition and there are many horsemen, myself included, who hold that a mare is the more genuine and courageous performer, particularly in the hunting field, a sport which, of course, takes place outside the mare's sexual cycle.

To be avoided is the 'rig', or cryptorchid, a male horse which has not been properly castrated because of the retention of a single testicle within the body. The result is for the horse to exhibit all the undesirable features of male behaviour: a rig is frankly an unmitigated nuisance when kept in company and it is unfortunate that the condition occurs more in ponies than in horses.

A buyer would be well-advised, therefore, to include amongst his questions one asking the vendor whether a horse has ever exhibited 'riggish' tendencies.

Stallions are not generally used in competitive sports in Europe, with the exception of dressage, although their use is common in Russia, the Middle and Far East and in Mediterranean countries also. A stallion is probably the most responsive, courageous and exciting of all equines to ride but, of course, there are some natural difficulties involved in keeping him with which many horse owners are not equipped to cope.

10 'Pony Suitable for a Child'

Don't give your son money. As far as you can afford it, give him horses.

Winston S. Churchill
My Early Life

The same general considerations apply to the buying of a child's pony as to the purchase of a horse, that is in terms of the factors involved. However, in acquiring a pony three parties are involved, excluding the vendor. They are the parents, the pony, of course, and the child; and it is largely upon the former that the success of the venture stands or falls. The great majority of children, however talented they may be in their own eyes or those of their parents, are not able to improve a pony or even maintain him at an existing level without adult supervision. Certainly, for a whole variety of reasons, like school work, exams and so on, they often cannot look after one without some help.

It follows then that the parents need to acquire some basis of knowledge before they take on the responsibility of a pony. I am not suggesting that parents must necessarily ride, but they should know enough to be able to give practical assistance, even if the knowledge has only been acquired from reading a book or two. It helps, too, and very significantly, if the child has been taught to ride by a good instructor before the purchase of a pony is even contemplated.

The object, that of obtaining a *suitable* pony, is a

responsibility which has to belong to the parents. (Pony-mad youngsters do not usually display a mature judgment in these matters, being only too ready to fall in love at first sight with any equine brought before them.)

If the parents are not horse-orientated the best way to acquire a pony for a child is, perhaps, to put the whole thing in qualified, professional hands, allowing the expert to find a pony suitable for the child's size, capability and temperament. If that is not practicable or the parents want to be more involved in the choice, there is no reason why they should not achieve a perfectly satisfactory outcome so long as they are prepared to apply themselves to the problem and so long as they recognise the pitfalls which exist.

One mistake, which is all too common, is for unknowledgeable parents, driven doubtless to desperation by their importunate offspring, to buy a very young pony in the starry-eyed but very mistaken belief that pony and child will 'grow up together'. They might, if the child survives or if it is not put off all things equine for ever, but it is not an experiment to be recommended.

Young ponies, and I mean those at three and four years old, not the immature babies of one and two, are just not suitable for inexperienced children and even less so if the parents are similarly inexpert. Young horses need capable experienced riders; whilst novice riders require older mounts who have learnt their business.

Another failing is for parents to be too ambitious for their children. As a result the child can be 'over-horsed' with an animal far beyond its modest capabilities. Jumping ponies of the tearaway variety, festooned with every gadget known to man, are prime examples. They may be just manageable by a strong, bold child, although I doubt whether they do anything to encourage good riding, but they are certainly not suitable for a beginner.

A Riding Pony of quality that is still sensible enough to carry a small
child safely

Not in the classic mould by any means but this pony has a look about
her and would make a good mount for a youngster

Most understandable is the naturally concerned
parent who buys a 'quiet' pony of indeterminate
background and shape. In its way such a pony can be
just as unsuitable. It may be all right for a toddler to sit
on and be led by Mum for a hundred yards down the
lane but for an older, rather more ambitious child, it can
be a source of awful frustration. We have all seen these
'quiet' ponies, so quiet that only a massive effort will
persuade the little creature to place one foot in front of
the other, being belaboured, mostly to little avail, by
small, scarlet-faced riders who have neither the strength
nor the experience to get them out of a reluctant walk.

Such an exercise again does nothing to improve the child's riding, if, indeed, it has anything to do with riding, and for the child it is hardly an enjoyable experience.

A 'first pony' for a small child must, of course, be quiet and reliable for the peace of mind of all concerned, but it does need to be reasonably responsive and willing if the child is going to enjoy her riding and to improve her ability.

As the child progresses, gets bigger and gains in confidence it should be possible to make a change to a pony that is, if anything, a little in advance of the child's capacity – something that provides a challenge, in fact. One should always, nonetheless, make sure that the pony relates to the physique of the rider. Fat ponies that spread the rider's upper thighs are an anathema and ones that are too big are quite beyond the effective control of small riders. Avoid, too, those with thick cresty necks. They are usually of the motor-on-regardless variety and are not suitable for youngsters.

British Native Ponies
In Britain we are enormously fortunate in having our nine native pony breeds as well as numerous derivatives whose antecedents may not be established but are for all that ponies of an order difficult to find elsewhere. Additionally, there are in Britain more opportunities for young people to ride and compete than anywhere else in the world.

The smaller native breeds are, in varying degrees, excellent ponies for young people. The Shetland is probably restricted on account of its size to the very small child, but the Welsh Mountain, the Welsh Pony, the Welsh Pony of Cob type, the Exmoor and Dartmoor are all first-rate ponies for children. They are tough, easily kept and manage very well on basic rations. Moreover they can be remarkably good performers.

It is true that the *Welsh Mountain Pony* may be just a shade too quick for an inexperienced child, but as they get older they steady down and are wonderful rides for small children. They stand at 12 hh or just under, they are intelligent and the best of performers. I have one, whose picture appears on p. 155, who was our children's first pony and is now with our latest god-daughter having taught no less than six families of children to ride and taken them all hunting, making sure he brought them back in one piece.

The *Welsh Pony* (Section B in the Stud Book) is the bigger of the two Welsh ponies. He comes up to 13.2 hh,

The very beautiful Welsh Mountain pony

The smaller of the Welsh Cobs, the Welsh Pony of Cob type, Section C, displaying the typical action of the breed

is of distinct riding type and because of his size has more scope as a performer. The third of the Welsh types is the *Welsh Pony of Cob type* (Section C). He, too, does not exceed 13.2 hh but is more stoutly built than the Section B and has the characteristic cob action. As a hunting/all-round pony for a keen child he is, I think, unsurpassed. Unlike the Section B, who can and does win Riding Pony show classes, he does not have the same showing potential, except in ridden classes for his breed, but he is a wonderful pony for children and light adults and virtually a natural jumper. What is more he is just as good in harness.

The modern *Dartmoor* is a quality riding pony which

does not exceed 12.2 hh. They jump and hunt and are, if anything, a shade less volatile than their Welsh equivalent.

The Welsh Pony Section B combines the native qualities with true riding type

The oldest of the native breeds is the *Exmoor*. He does not exceed 12.3 hh and if properly handled and made, which is not, alas, always the case, is the toughest of hunting ponies and exceptionally versatile.

The great advantage of these native ponies is their ability to live out throughout the year and to thrive on basic rations. Additionally, they are inherently sound, rarely sick or sorry and they are full of pony character. By which I mean they have an in-born intelligence and sagacity denied to the larger equines.

A champion Dartmoor. The breed, either in its pure form or when crossed with a small Thoroughbred or Riding Pony, is an ideal source of quality children's pony

When children need larger ponies there are always the admirable Connemaras and New Forests, both of which are performers at the highest level.

Additionally, of course, there are the part-bred ponies, many of them of what we now call Working Hunter Pony type. These, with, I think, the Connemaras and New Forest, are the ideal transitional mounts between ponies and horses for young people.

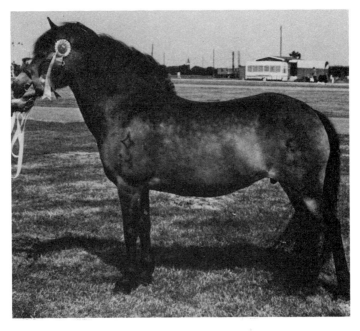

The oldest of the British native breeds is the hardy Exmoor

This transition to a horse after riding a sure-footed, sensible pony whose stride is sufficiently short to be easily adjusted to the circumstance, is a difficult period for young riders. Too big a horse, with too long a stride, is sometimes over much for a young rider, who loses confidence as a result. The ideal, in my view, is a working hunter type with a background of native blood standing around 15 hh.

In ponies, as in horses, conformation which contributes to a natural balance is a paramount requirement. No child will learn to ride well on a badly balanced, ill-made pony which is limited in its performance potential by reason of its physical structure.

Excellent example of a working hunter pony

So far as ponies are concerned I believe that age is less of a consideration. A pony goes on operating satisfactorily for some years more than a horse and is not subject to nearly so many ailments. A 12-year-old pony will most likely have half his working life in front of him and, of course, he has the experience to cope with the inadequacies of his young rider.

If one is concerned with winning rosettes in the show ring there is a multitude of the most beautiful riding ponies to be had. In fact, the Riding Pony, a uniquely British product based on the judicious crossing of native and Thoroughbred blood, is possibly the most perfectly proportioned equine in the world. He inherits the fire, the elegance, the refinement and floating action of the Thoroughbred in full, although he also has the drawbacks associated with that high-bred aristocrat. He is highly-strung, more delicate in constitution and less able to live rough than his more down-to-earth native brothers and is, frankly, less versatile and utilitarian for the child who wants to do a bit of everything and go to the Pony Club camp as well.

The author's Welsh Mountain Pony Muffin, who has taught six families of children to ride

In conclusion let it be remembered that though there are quite a lot of ponies who, through no fault of their own, are not entirely suitable for children, there are many more children (and parents) who are unsuitable for ponies.

11   A Creature of Instinct

From the Gods comes the saying Know Thyself
Juvenal, *Satires* XI, 27
(inscribed in the Temple at Delphi)

To 'know thyself' may be an impossible precept for
man, although infinitely desirable. In the context of
horse-keeping, however, it is essential that we try to
know something not only of ourselves but of the horses
which become our responsibility. If we were to erect at
our British Equestrian Centre, or indeed at any such
centre in the world, a temple to the horse, we ought to
incise deeply into the stonework a parody of that
Delphic inscription. It would read 'Know Thy Horse'.
Knowing, or understanding, the limitations of the
horse's mentality, will not, perhaps, help us to buy the
right horse but it may well ensure that having bought
one the partnership thus entered into has a chance of
being successful.

The necessity of being able to appreciate the horse in
physical terms and being able to relate the mechanics of
the physical structure to the purposes required of it is
not difficult to understand; less emphasis, however, is
given in our training systems to an application of the
make-up of the horse's personality and the workings of
his limited mental process, one which is so contrary to
our own. To understand the horse's mind is, in fact, just
as important as knowing about the mechanics of his
movement.

The training of a horse is concerned with a two-fold approach: one has to do with the build-up of the physical capacity and the other with the mental development and the extension of the animal's limited powers of concentration. Neither can nor should be neglected in the production of the 'whole' horse, for performance is as much the result of mental attitudes as of physical ability.

If, therefore, the horse we buy is to be a satisfactory acquisition it must be essential that we understand the whole of him, not just his physical aspects.

To a degree we may all be guilty of anthromorphism, whether it is with our dogs, who are all too easily regarded as four-legged members of the human family; or with our horses, whom we may expect to respond in human, or even doggy, terms.

Of course, horses are neither human nor canine. They are equine and their actions are motivated and conditioned by quite different backgrounds, and by instinct rather than by reason, which remains the human prerogative.

Once we can appreciate that then we begin to understand what sometimes seems to be paradoxical behaviour in our equine partners.

The root of horse behaviour lies in the fact that the horse is a non-aggressive herbivorous herd animal who, despite thousands of years of domestication, is still largely governed by deeply-ingrained instincts pertaining to his feral life, whilst deriving particular characteristics from his dependence upon humans, who have, in most instances, taken the place of the dominant herd leader. The personality is completed by the senses which are common to all creatures.

It is as a result of this background that the horse developed a set of very efficient defence mechanisms to ensure his survival. He has extraordinarily sensitive powers of sight, hearing and smell, a highly developed sixth sense, and the physique which enables him to move swiftly away from danger or from the threat of danger. That there is little need for so advanced a defence system in his domesticated role is not something we can expect the horse to appreciate. He retains all those old instincts and remains what he has always been, an essentially nervous and highly-strung animal.

In the feral state the equine life was dominated by the constant search for food and the continual awareness of the need to avoid natural dangers and predators. At certain times of the year the reproductive urge became of paramount importance. These are factors which still colour his life today, even if food is usually plentiful and obtainable without effort and when danger is remote.

Possibly as important a facet of the horse's personality is his memory. His powers of reason are not high, if indeed they exist, but his memory is as long and retentive as that of the proverbial elephant.

Someone once wrote that when we deal with horses 'we carve on stone and what is written can never be effaced'. Of course, we make use of the memory in training the horse but whilst he remembers those things which he associates with pleasure and reward, he also remembers the unpleasant experiences. This last is not a bad thing since if the horse misbehaves and is corrected immediately he associates the misdemeanour with whatever retribution was meted out. If, for instance, a horse kicks at a hound in the hunting field and for his sins receives a couple of sharp cuts round his backside he associates the action of kicking with punishment and the extreme displeasure of his rider. So long as the punishment is delivered almost before the offending hoof has returned to the ground it is unlikely that he will repeat the experiment. It would, of course, be no use at all if he was taken home and then given a good beating for his misbehaviour. There is no way in which he could possibly understand the reason for the beating and reasonably enough he would be resentful and soured by treatment which he could not relate to the action. What is more, he would remember and might then become a rather unpleasant individual unless some more intelligent human could regain his confidence. You can beat a boy for stealing apples hours, or even days, after the event and he will know why he is being punished, but you can't do that with a horse.

The highly-strung nature of the horse can also present problems. Because the first line of defence is flight, instant and unthinking, the horse, often to the exasperation of his rider, will shy violently at the leaf that flutters in a hedge or the piece of paper lying on the verge, and the fitter he is the more likely he is to spook at such things and to do so more violently. Reassured, he will draw courage from his rider and go on. In fact, if he trusts his rider it is amazing what he will pass (or, for that matter, jump). If, however, his rider should be so insecure as to jab his mouth when he shies, or so impatient and unthinking as to hit him it will only serve to confirm his fear and matters go from bad to worse.

Similarly, whilst it would be quite untrue to say that horses never bolt with their riders and foolish to deny that some horses in their anxiety to get on, or because they are excited, will not take a rather stronger hold than is exactly comfortable, much of the problem with the horse that takes off is attributable to the rider and the pain to which he is subjecting the horse as a result of his inexpert hands. If the horse experiences pain in his mouth because of a severe bit or even a fairly mild one that is mishandled, he is more likely to increase his speed in an effort to escape from the discomfort than to do otherwise. It is, after all, in his nature to do so. How often does one see a child, or an adult, endeavouring to

lead a horse or pony into a box or trailer by facing the
animal and pulling with all their weight on the reins or
lead rope. The reaction of the horse, the natural one, is
to pull back, and since he is the stronger of the two he
usually wins.

Mind you, this innate sensitivity due in the
herbivorous animal to a low pain tolerance is used to
further our ends in training the horse, since he will
always *go away* from pain or from the fear of it, even if
pain is in reality no more than the slightest of
discomforts. Allied to repetition and a system of
minimal discomfort followed by immediate reward
when a response is obtained, this curious quality
actually helps in training the horse. If in the stable we
tap a horse on the flank while holding his head he moves
his quarters away from the tap. Later he will learn to
move his quarters away from the action of the single leg
applied in roughly the same place.

We teach horses to obey the signals we are pleased to
call the aids through repetition certainly, but also by a
system of what might be termed reward and minimal
discomfort. Horses, of course, have to be taught these
signals made by the rider and to learn what response is
required to them. They were not, however, born
understanding that pressure from the legs is a request to
go forward nor, we should remember, do they read
books. We know what is wanted of the horse but he does
not – until we teach him.

By closing our legs on the horse we are imposing the
smallest of discomforts. Initially, it means nothing to
him and we may get no result at all until an assistant
walks up behind him and encourages him to go forward.
When that happens the legs cease to squeeze and we
make much of the horse so that he begins to understand
that we are pleased with him for going forward. By
repetition he soon learns what the squeezing legs mean

and that when he obeys he is rewarded by their ceasing to be applied.

The gregarious nature of the horse, the herd instinct, can also be used to our advantage but it can also be exasperating on occasions. Horses when in company with their own kind will always go with more enthusiasm than when they are on their own and they will very often jump fences which they would otherwise decline most firmly. They will also jump an obstacle if by doing so they can rejoin their comrades, the herd, and conversely they may be considerably more reluctant about jumping if asked to leave the herd and jump away from them.

Indeed, there was the well-documented instance of the cavalry squadron in the Boer War wishing to send a trooper from its ranks with a message. To the consternation of all it was found that no horse could be persuaded to leave his companions!

The desire to join other horses (as well as a thousand other reasons) may cause the horse to become excited – something which he does all too easily. When he becomes very excited he may momentarily forget his lessons and then he becomes out of the rider's control.

The herd also represented security (as did the cavalry squadron to its individual members) and horses need to feel secure just as much as we humans.

In the domestic state horses may not live in even a herd of two or three but may be kept singly. What occurs then, in, I think, either instance, is for the horse to regard his familiar surroundings, and particularly the box in which he is fed, as the centre of his security. Much of it has to do with the provision of food, which remains an overriding obsession in the equine mind, but the security involved exerts a great influence on the horse. The stable (and the food) has an undeniable gravitational pull. Horses always stride out when going home. If you are unwise enough to have a schooling area too near to the stable the horse almost always hangs towards the latter.

From that there are lessons to be learnt. For instance, when getting a horse used to traffic one would go out down the quiet lanes and return by the busier roads when the horse's mind will be more concerned with getting back to the stable and food than with the traffic passing him. Quite frequently when horses change hands they will display symptoms of insecurity, behaving uncharacteristically until they have had time to settle in their new surroundings.

Security, also, has much to do with the dependence upon the human, who takes the place of the dominant animal in the herd. This does, however, depend upon the nature of the individual horse. Most horses in a herd are followers, willing and indeed anxious to be led, but there will also be dominant horses, either mares or stallions, who will be group leaders within the herd.

The dominant horse remains dominant in domestication and will attempt to dominate the human who cares for him and rides him. These are usually the bold, courageous horses which succeed in competition. They may, because of their high courage, have some temper as well. If they are to realise their considerable potential they do need a little careful handling.

The human reaction is often to respond by attempting to be more dominant than the dominant horse, and it doesn't work. The horse has to be allowed to think that he dominates if we are to avoid a continual and non-productive battle. We have to obtain results by the employment of a little guile, letting the horse *think* that he is doing what he wanted to do.

The subservient horse, on the other hand, needs to draw confidence from his human and rather than coaxing (which we might do with the dominant fellow) he will benefit from firm no-nonsense treatment —

which, of course, is what he wants and needs.

In the end you may think that the easiest thing about owning a horse is buying him.

Index

Page numbers in *italic* refer to the illustrations